AF575607

SHAM SHUI PO
深水埗
UTTERS
AND
PRINCE EDWA
太子
Sham Mong Rd
MONG KOK
旺角
CHARMING
GARDEN
富榮花園
KING
YAU MA
油麻地
KWUN CHUN
官涌
TSIM SHA
SAI YING PUN
西營盤
MID-LEVELS
半山區
半山
CENTRAL
中環
Queensway
WA
Map data ©2023 Google

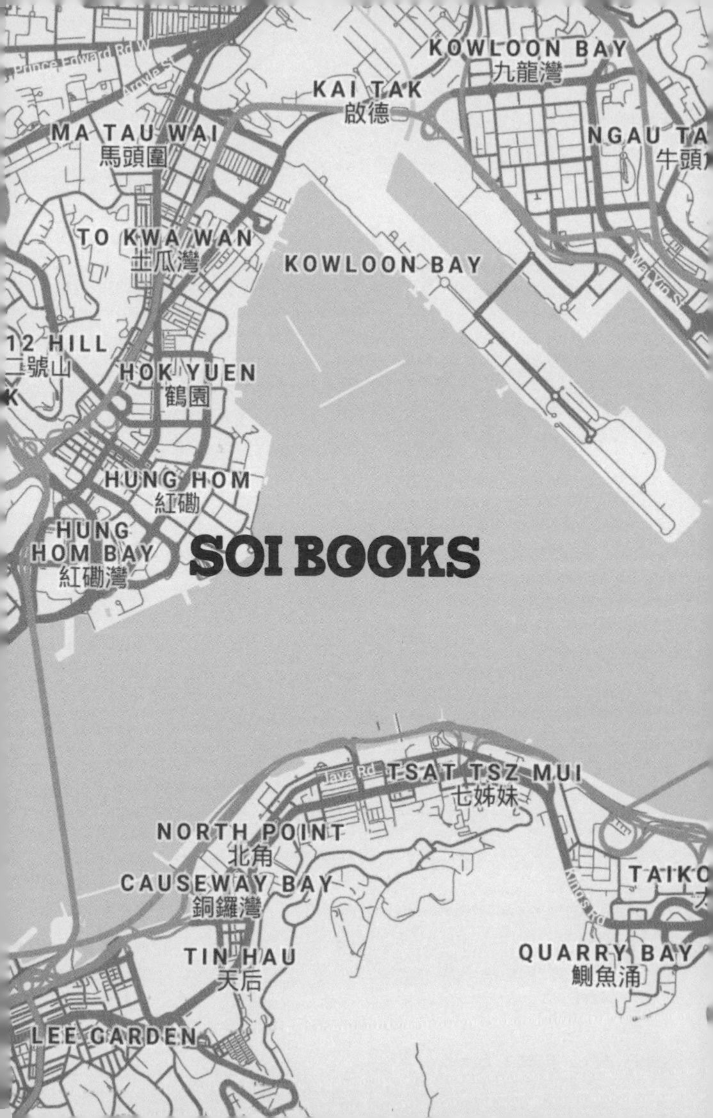
Prince Edward Rd W
Argyle St
KOWLOON BAY
九龍灣
KAI TAK
啟德
MA TAU WAI
馬頭圍
TO KWA WAN
土瓜灣
KOWLOON BAY
Wai Yip St
HOK YUEN
鶴園
HUNG HOM
紅磡
HUNG HOM BAY
紅磡灣
SOI BOOKS
Java Rd
TSAT TSZ MUI
七姊妹
NORTH POINT
北角
CAUSEWAY BAY
銅鑼灣
King's Rd
TIN HAU
天后
QUARRY BAY
鰂魚涌
LEE GARDEN

Soi Books / Stickerbomb Ltd

Design and layout by Ryo Sanada,
Suridh Hassan and XEME.

ISBN: 978-1-7397509-0-9
Printed in the U.K.

@bombstagram
www.stickerbombworld.com
www.soibooks.com

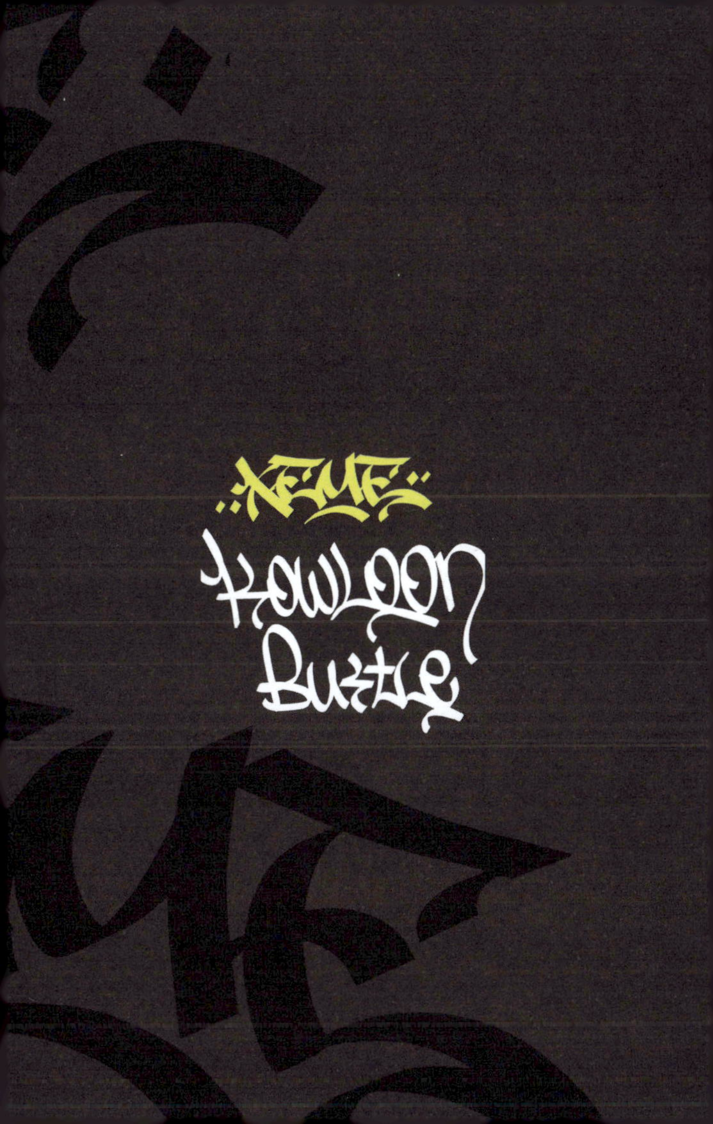
Kowloon
Bustle

八龍

鴉巢山、筆架山、獅子山、雞胸山
慈雲山、大老山、東山、飛鵝山

Map data ©2021 Goo

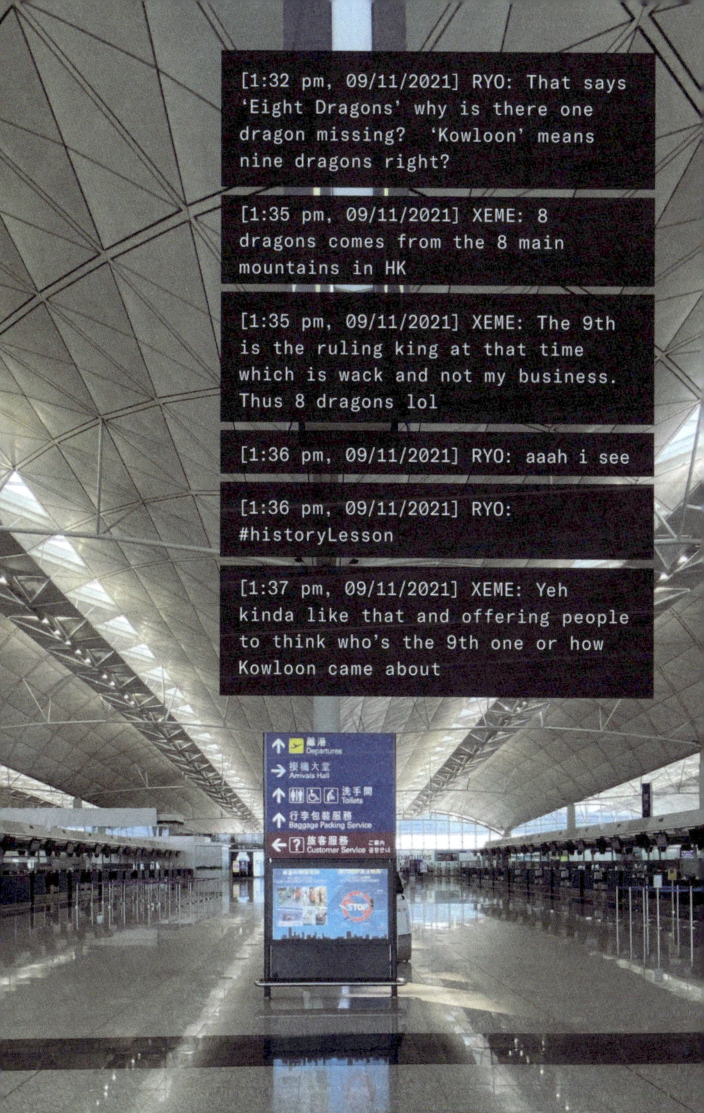

[1:32 pm, 09/11/2021] RYO: That says 'Eight Dragons' why is there one dragon missing? 'Kowloon' means nine dragons right?

[1:35 pm, 09/11/2021] XEME: 8 dragons comes from the 8 main mountains in HK

[1:35 pm, 09/11/2021] XEME: The 9th is the ruling king at that time which is wack and not my business. Thus 8 dragons lol

[1:36 pm, 09/11/2021] RYO: aaah i see

[1:36 pm, 09/11/2021] RYO: #historyLesson

[1:37 pm, 09/11/2021] XEME: Yeh kinda like that and offering people to think who's the 9th one or how Kowloon came about

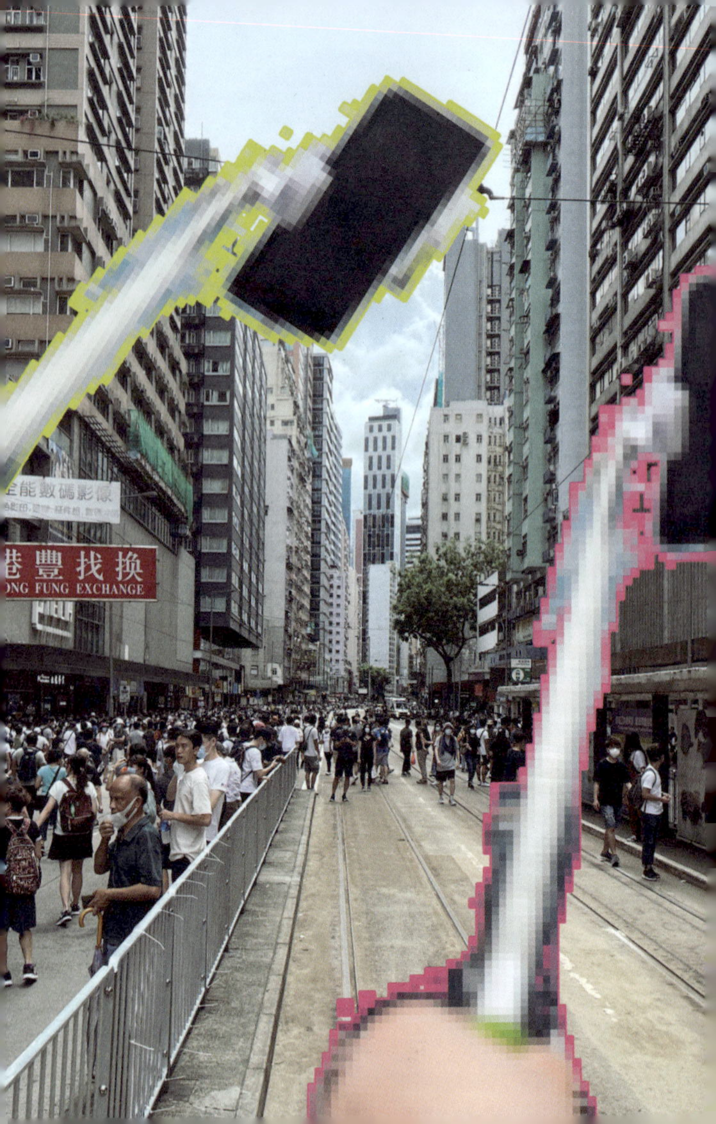
能數碼影像
港豐找換
ONG FUNG EXCHANGE

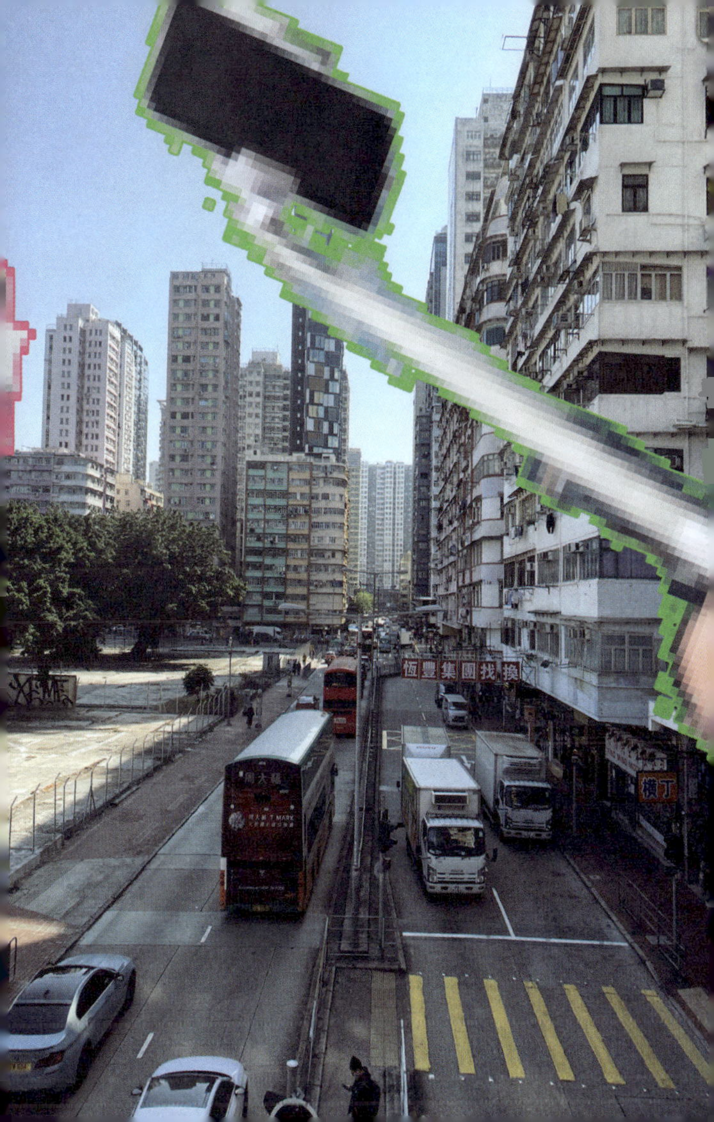
恆豐集團找換
橫丁

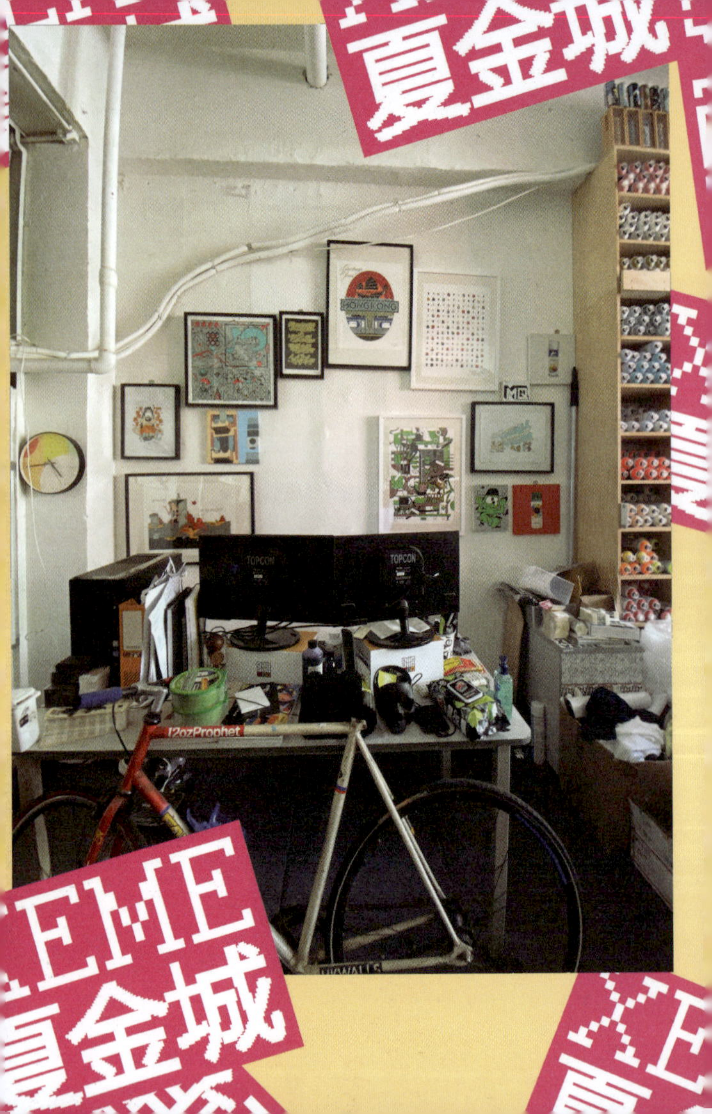
夏金城
HONGKONG
TOPCON
TOPCON
12ozProphet
EME
夏金城

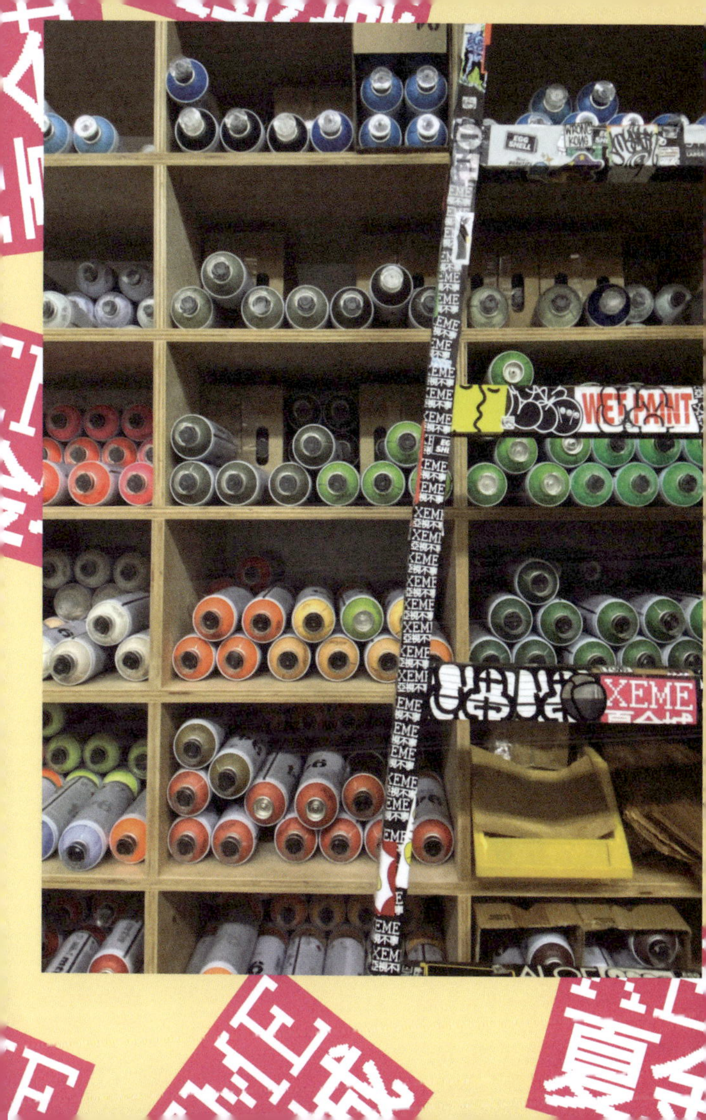
WET PAINT
XEME

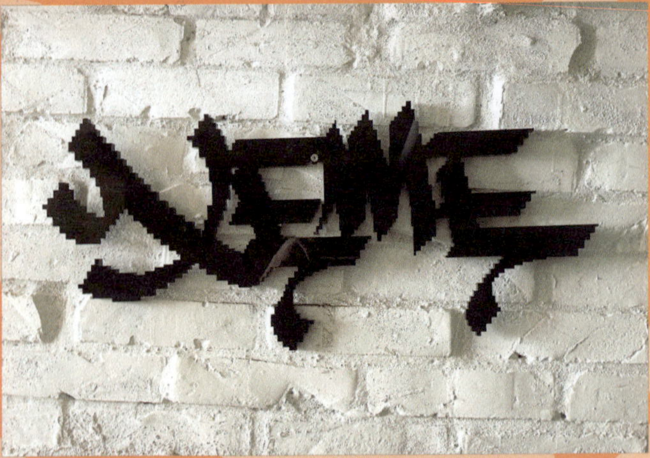

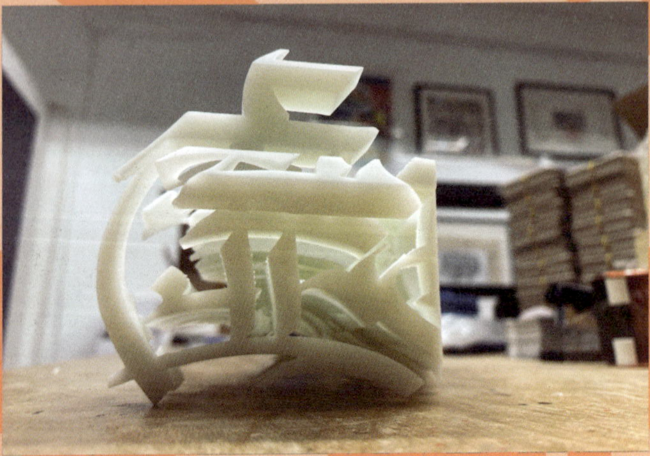

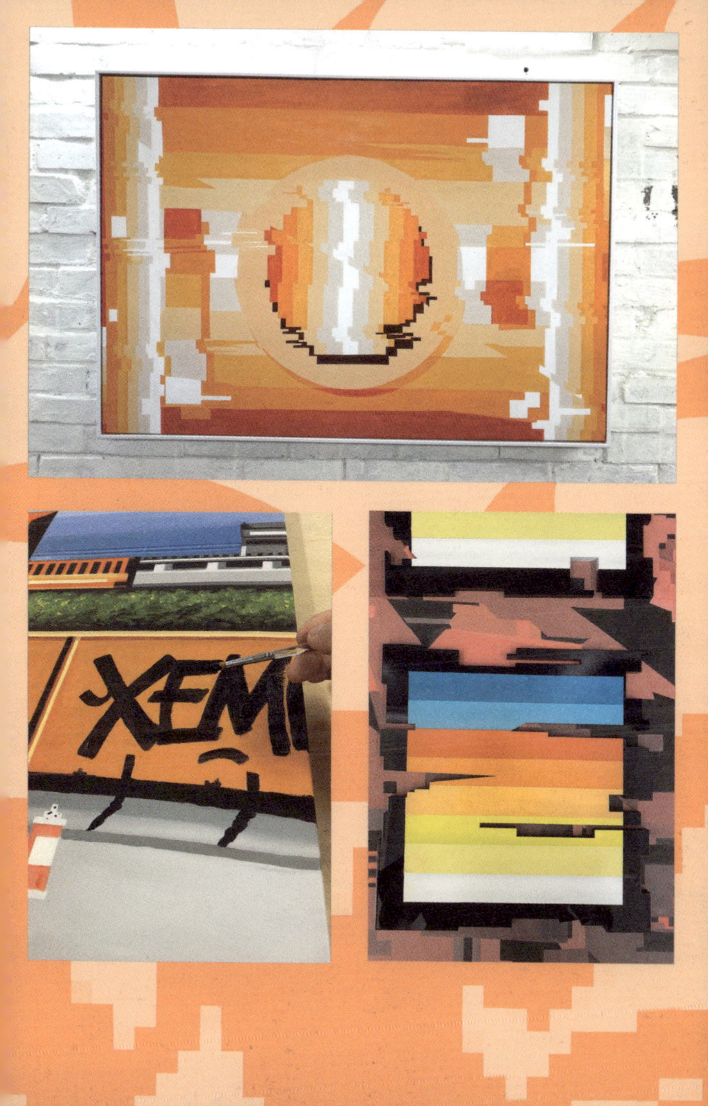
XEM

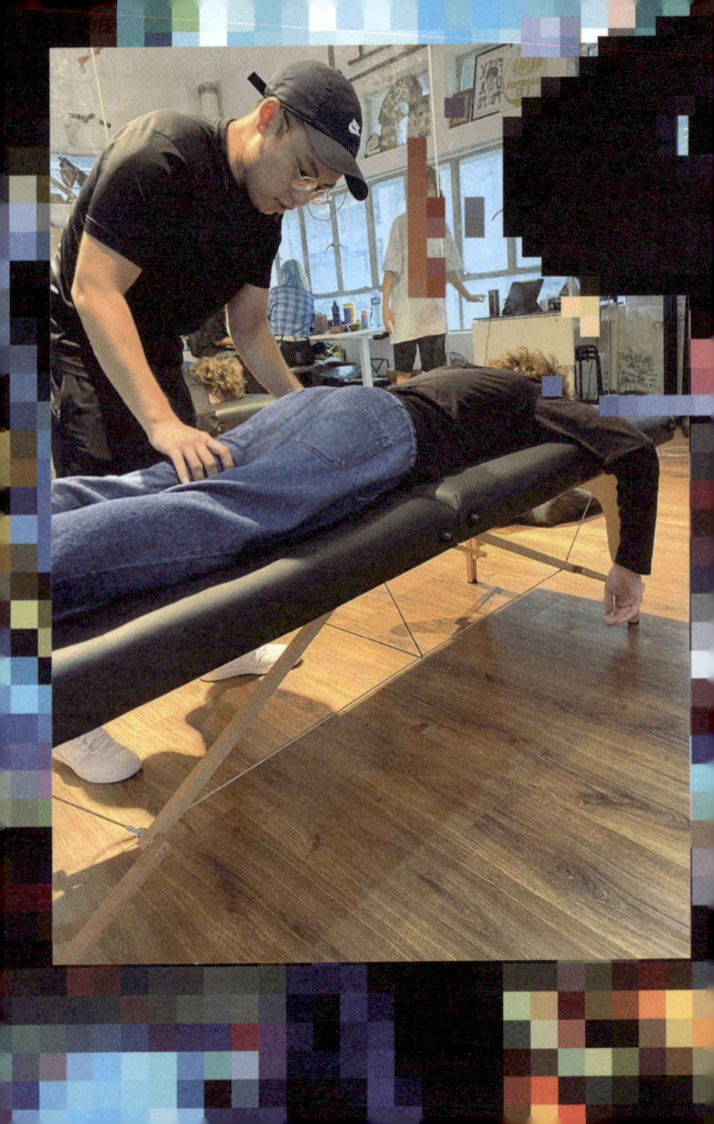

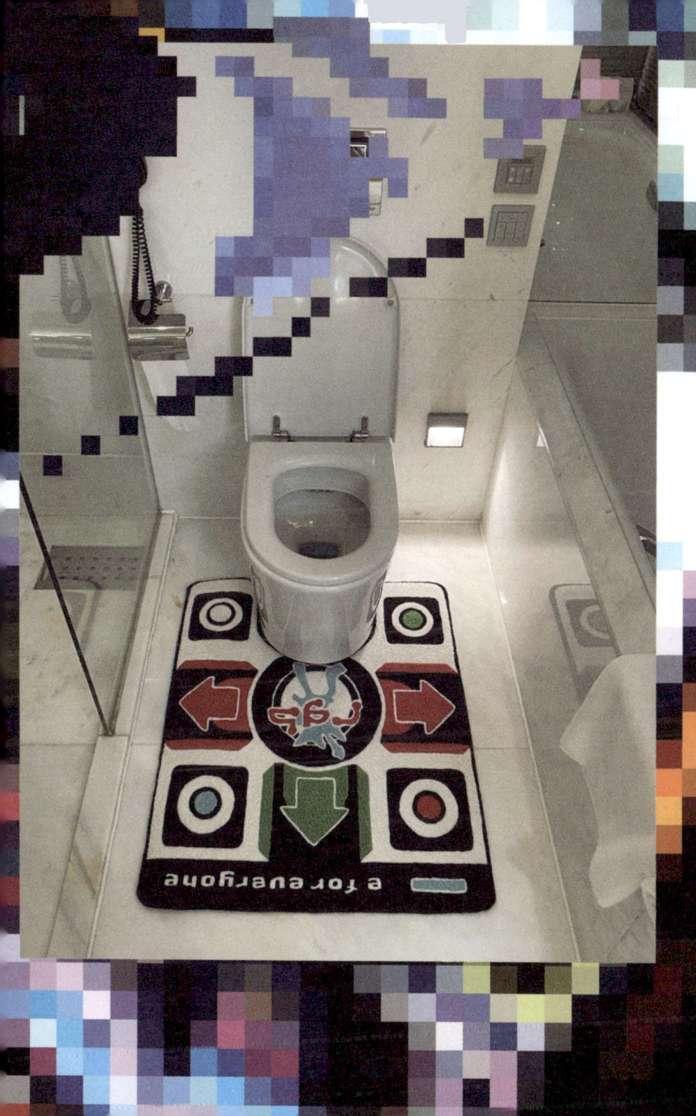
e for everyone

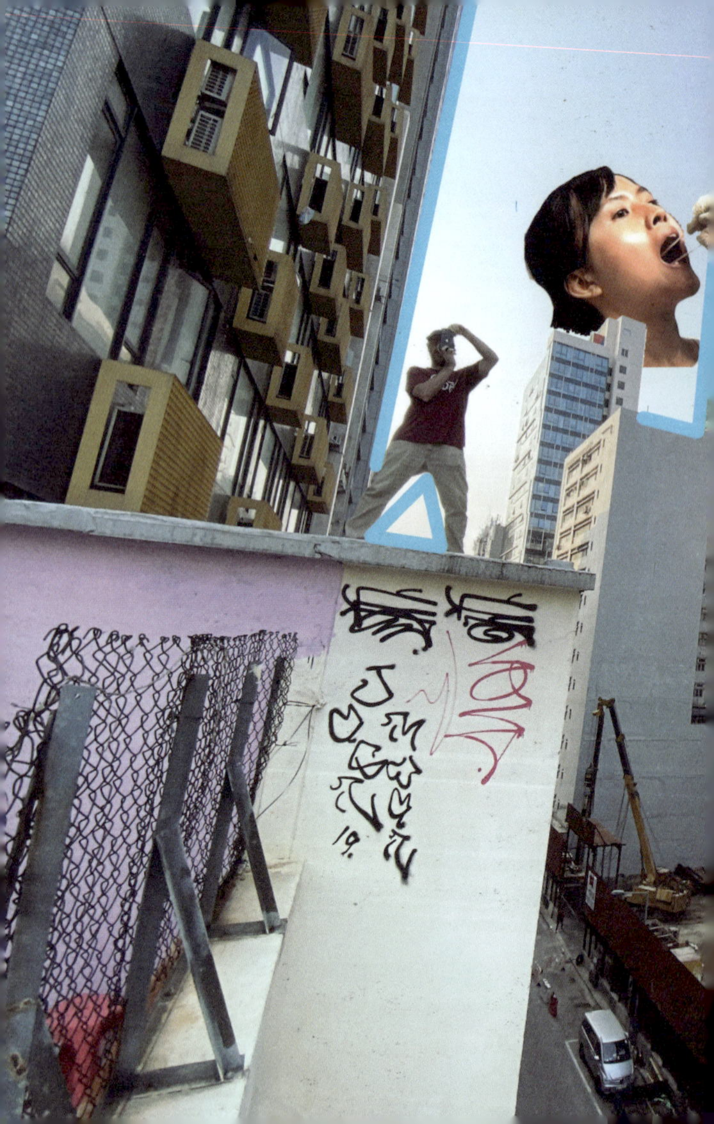

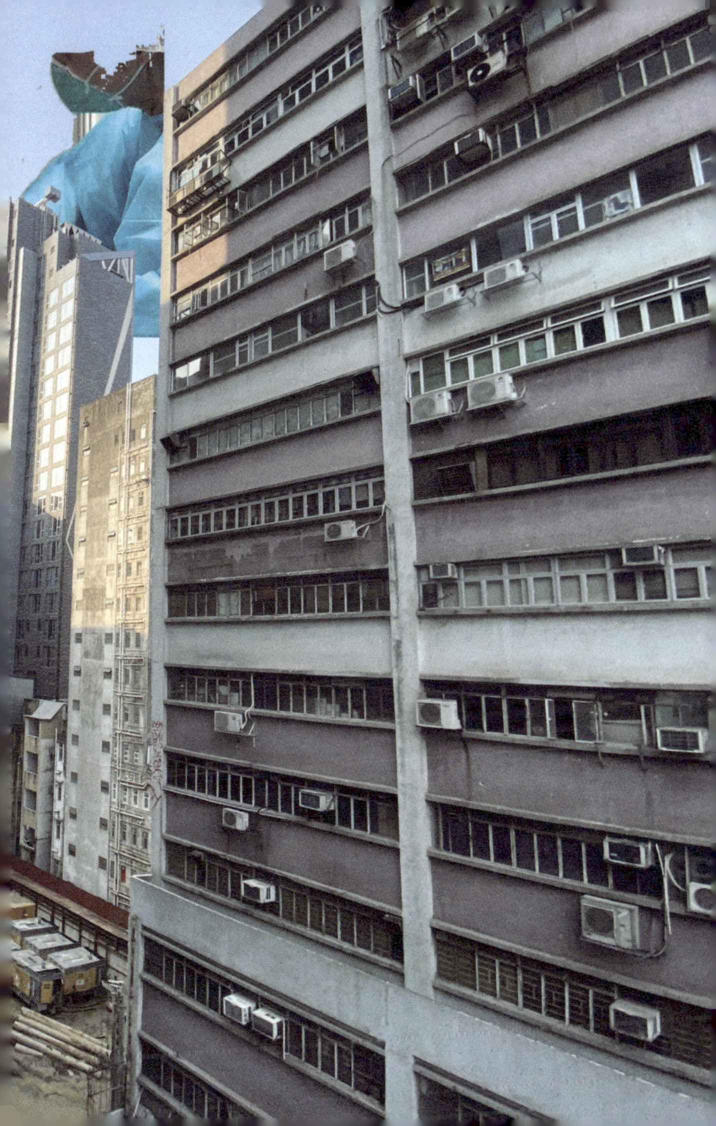

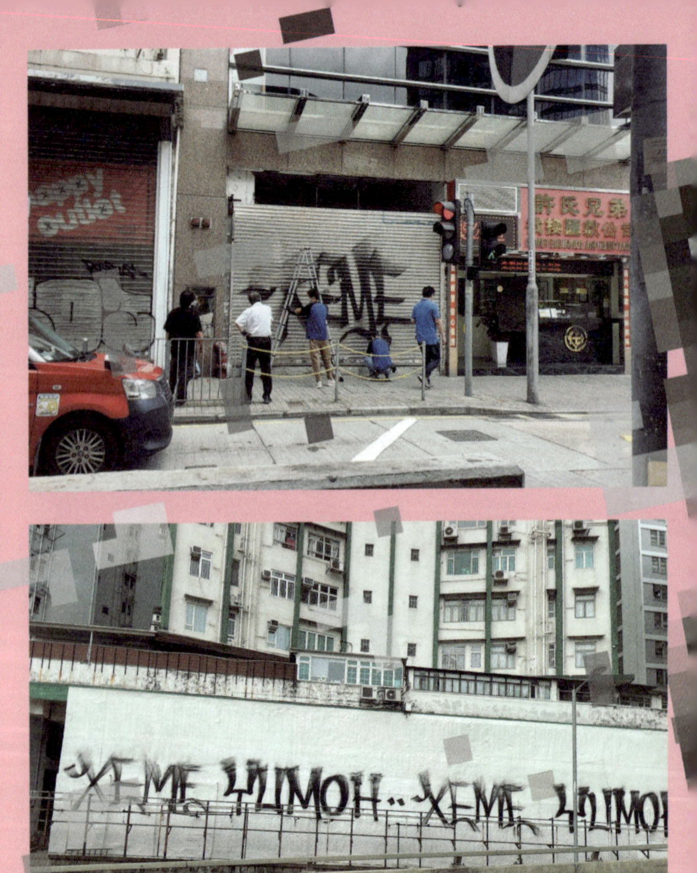

[9:55 am, 08/12/2021] RYO: Ok, here's the big question that everyone wants to know - how has HK changed over the last few years?

[9:57 am, 08/12/2021] XEME: Not that great politics wise. The pandemic really helped the gov to keep people quiet and staying indoors. And obviously they've been blatantly passing laws and stuff that shuts people with an opposing opinion down

[9:57 am, 08/12/2021] RYO: How has all this affected the work you and other artists do?

[10:03 am, 08/12/2021] XEME: Actually I think more people that start doing graffiti out of the movement. But the people around me are pretty much the same.

[10:06 am, 08/12/2021] RYO: Do you think the public opinion on art, murals, graffiti in the streets has changed?

[10:12 am, 08/12/2021] XEME: A little at the midst of the protest when people thought we're doing political graffiti but not that much anymore.

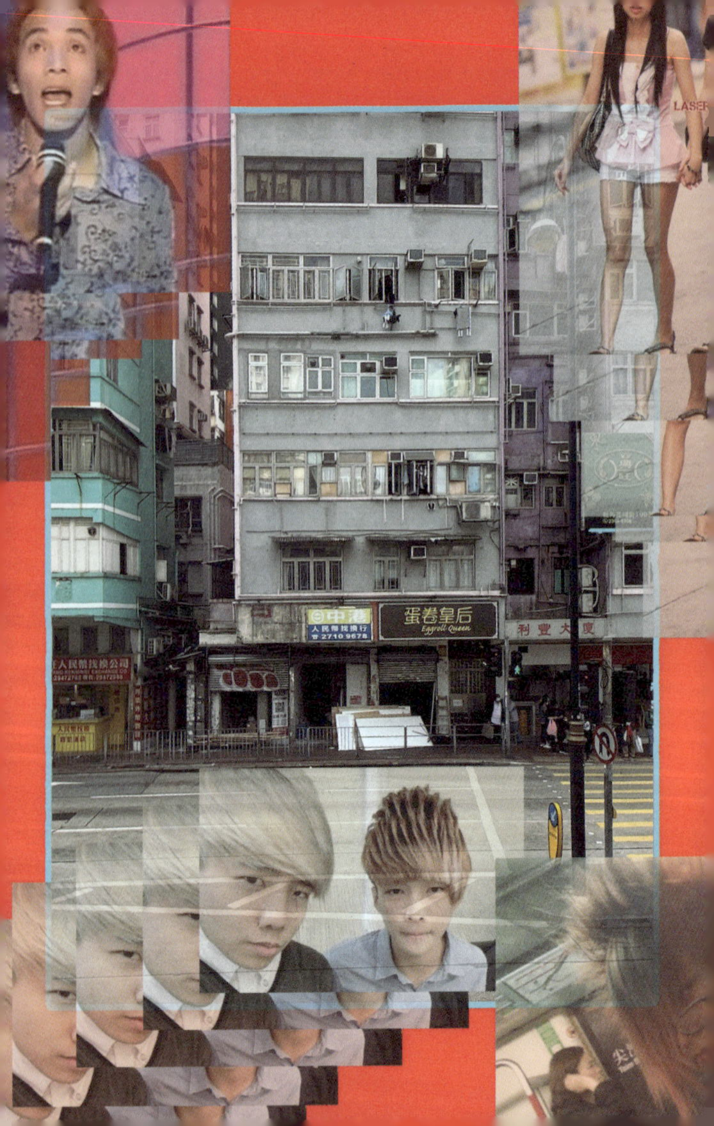
中港
人民幣找換行
2710 9678
蛋卷皇后
Eggroll Queen
利豐大廈

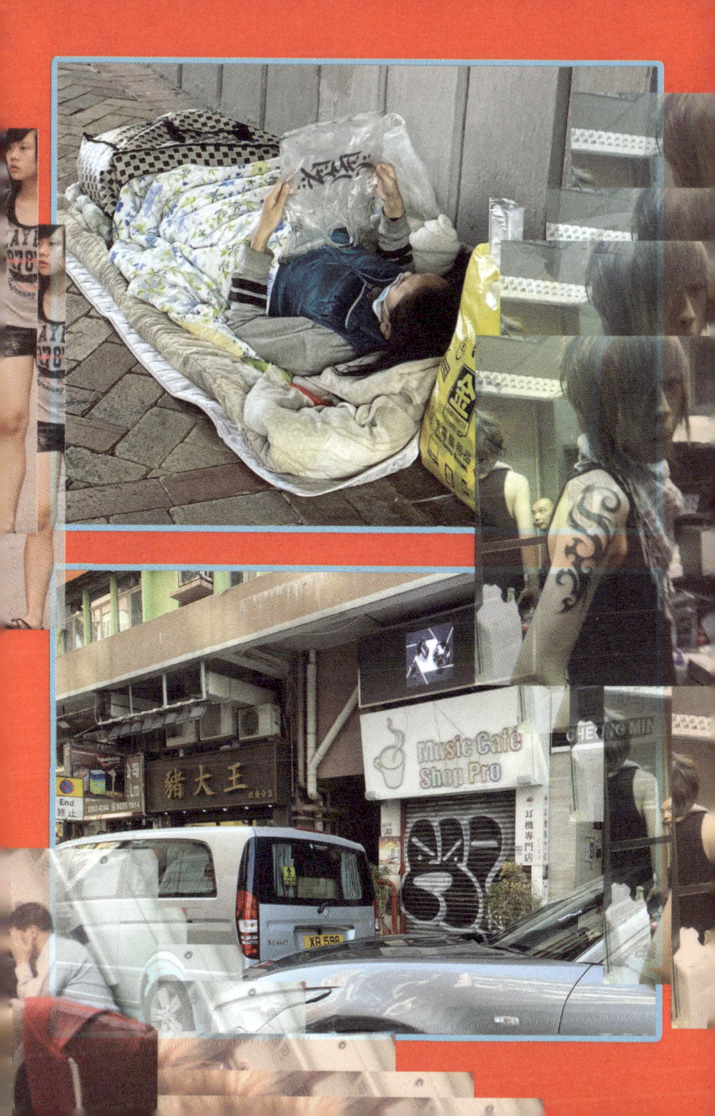
豬大王
End
終止
Music Café
Shop Pro
耳機專門店
XR 588

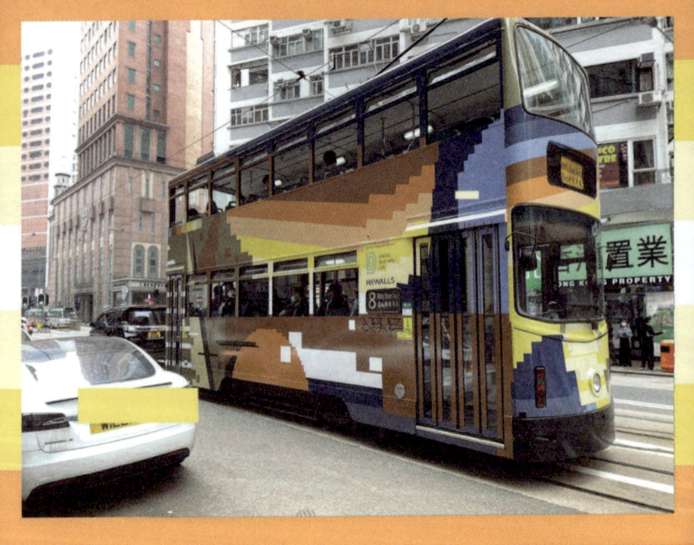
HKWALLS
置業
PROPERTY

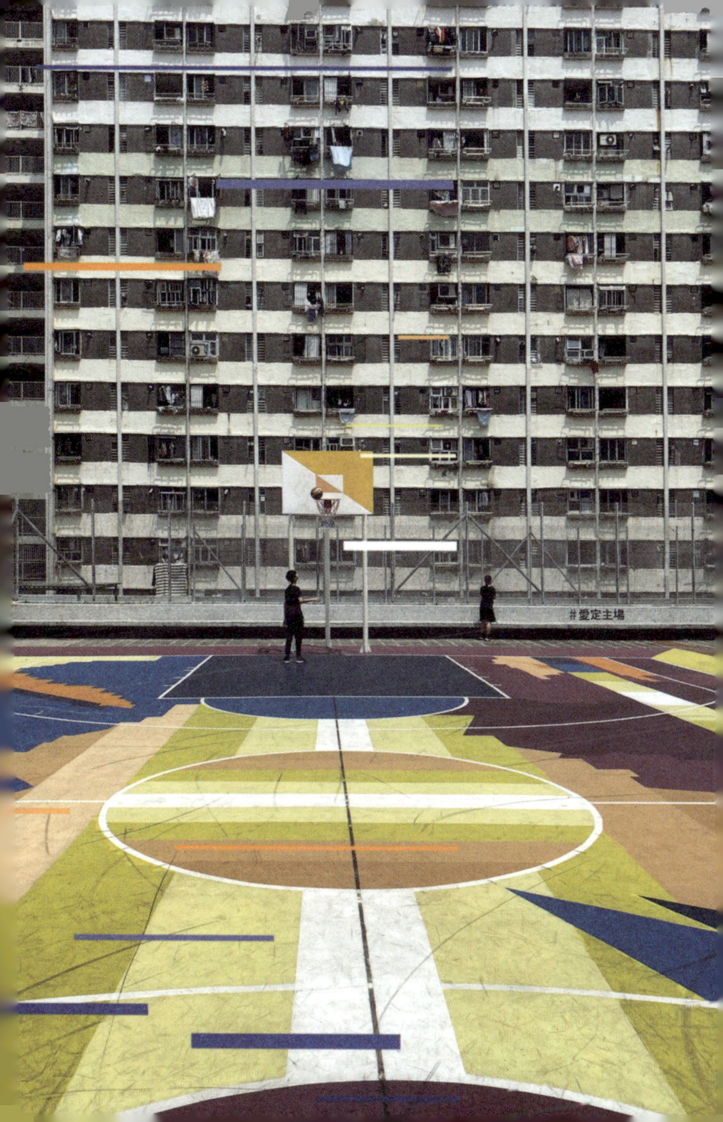
#愛定主場

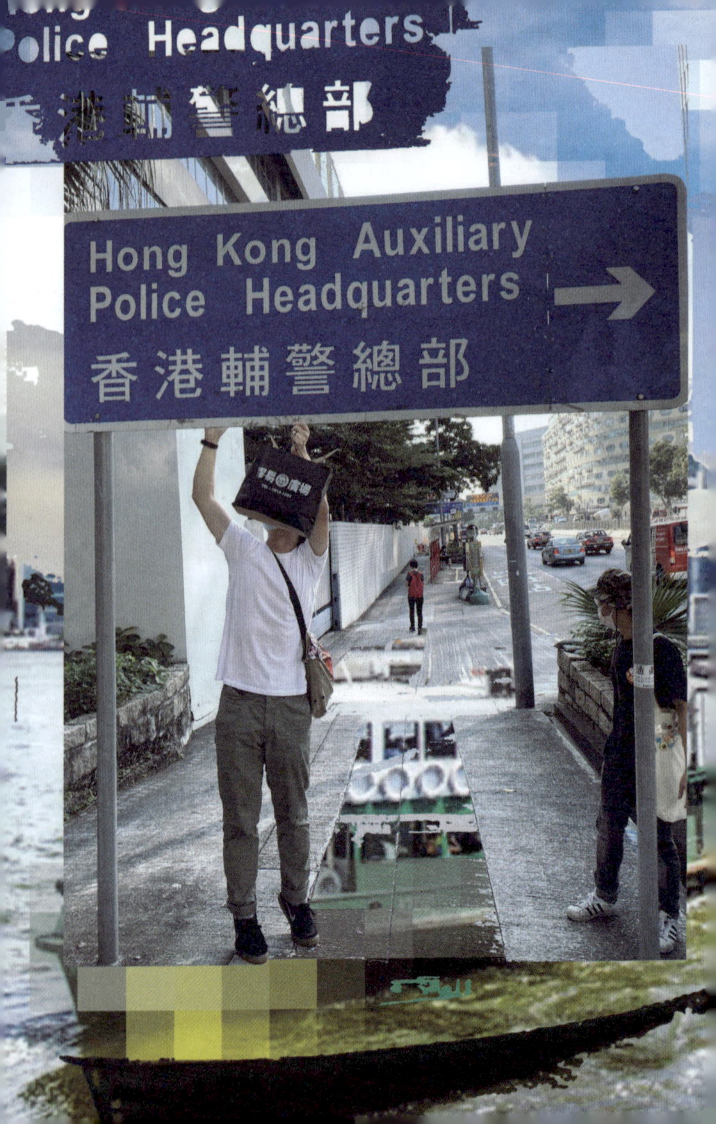

Police Headquarters
Hong Kong Auxiliary
Police Headquarters
香港輔警總部

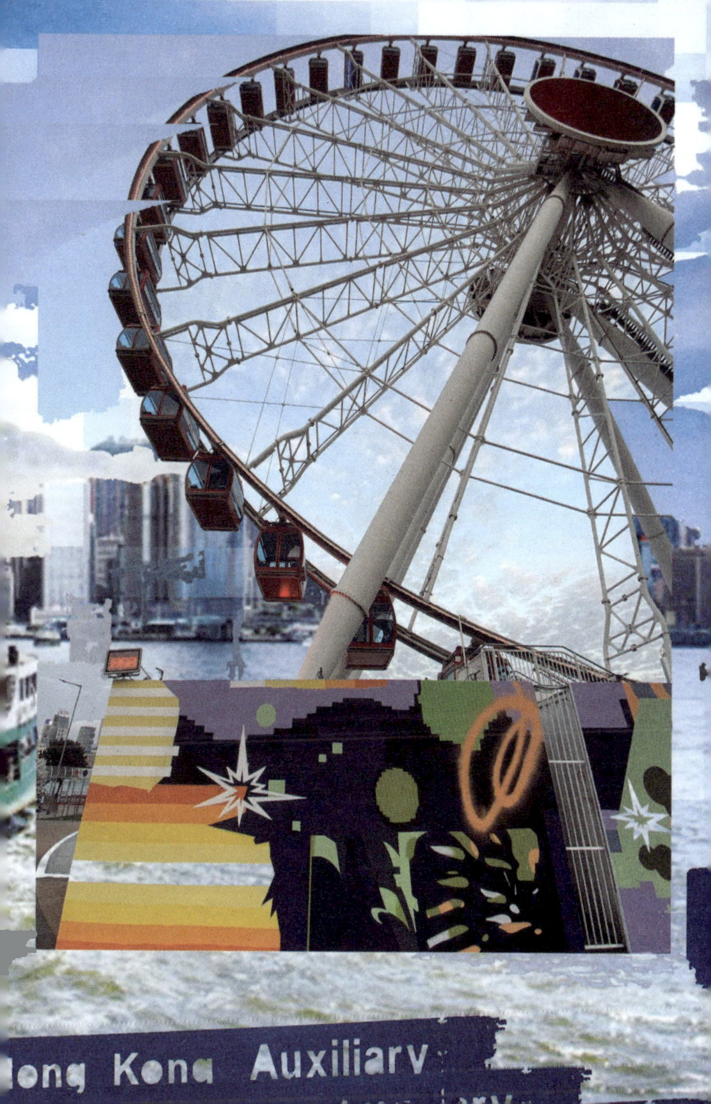
ong Kong Auxiliary

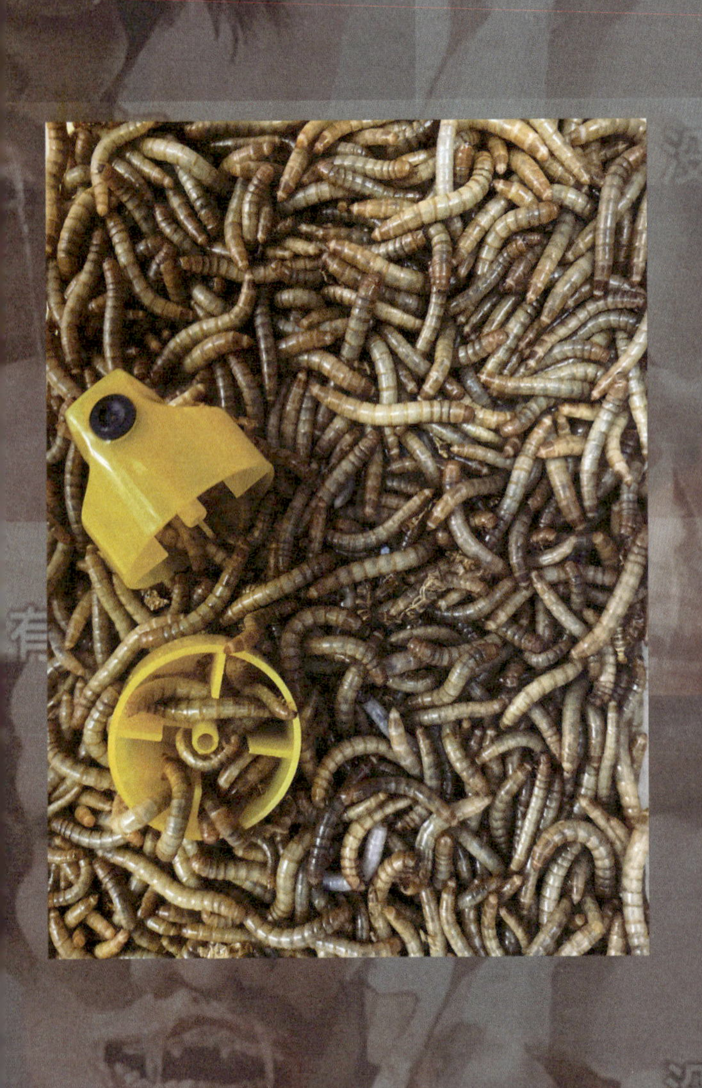

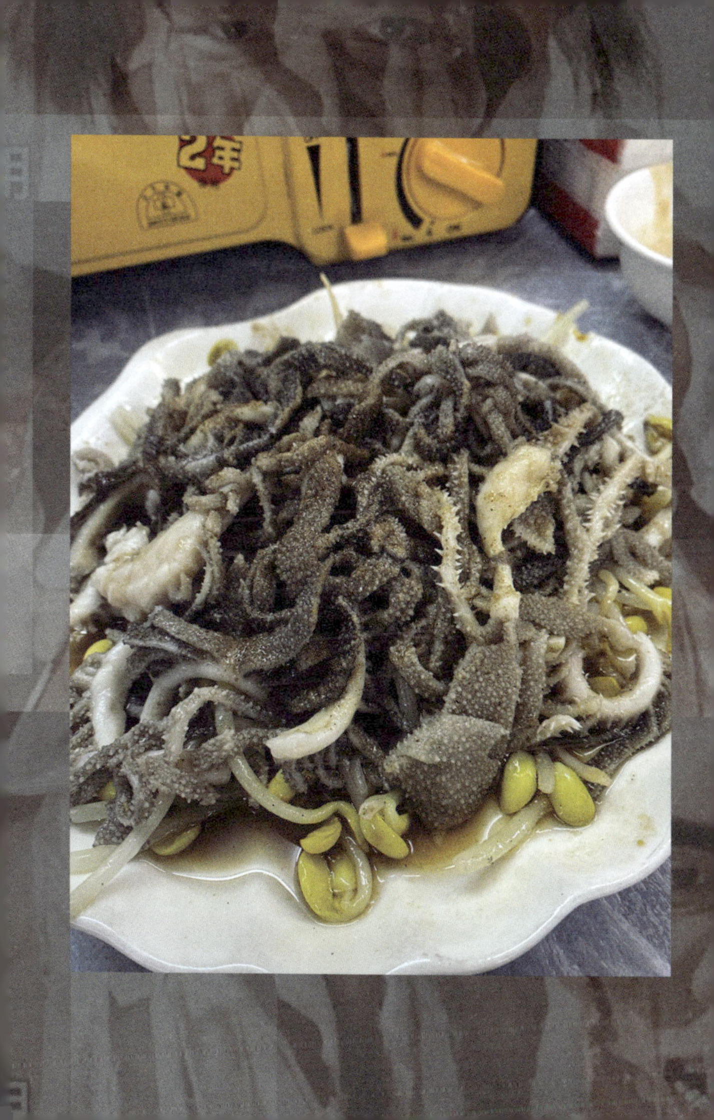

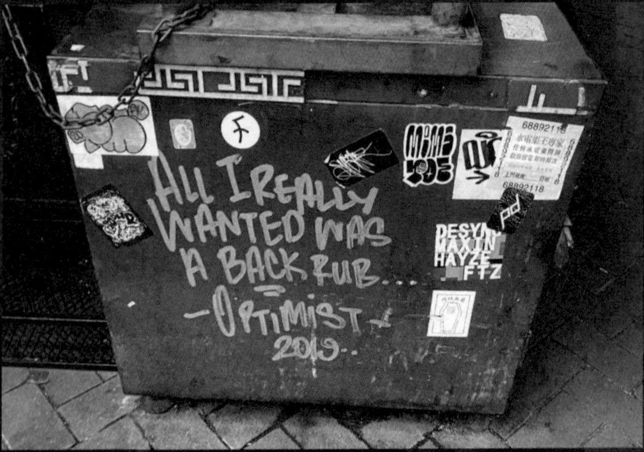

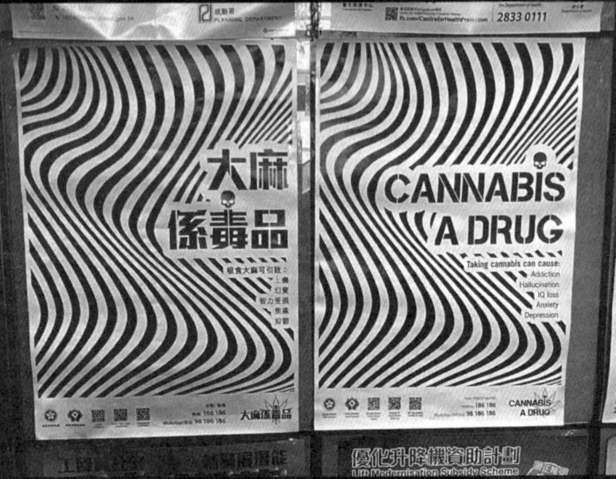

PLANNING DEPARTMENT
fb.com/CentreforHealthProtection
2833 0111
大麻
係毒品
吸食大麻可引致：
上癮
幻覺
智力受損
焦慮
抑鬱
CANNABIS
A DRUG
Taking cannabis can cause:
Addiction
Hallucination
IQ loss
Anxiety
Depression
186 186
98 186 186
大麻係毒品
CANNABIS
A DRUG
優化升降機資助計劃
Lift Modernisation Subsidy Scheme

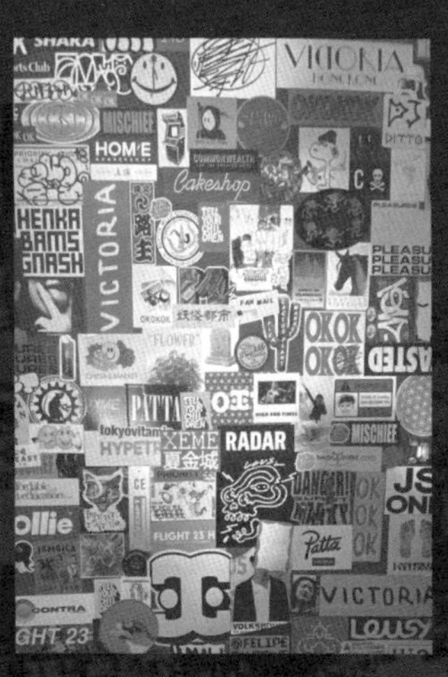
SHAKA
MISCHIEF
HOME
COMMONWEALTH
Cakeshop
VICTORIA
PLEASURES
OKOK
WASTED
PATTA
tokyovitamin
HYPETRAK
XEME
夏金城
RADAR
DANGER!
ollie
FLIGHT 23
CONTRA
Patta
VICTORIA
LOUSY

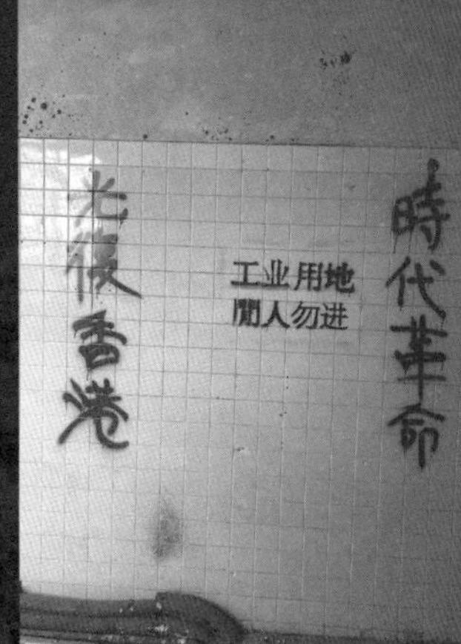
時代革命
工业用地
閒人勿进
光復香港

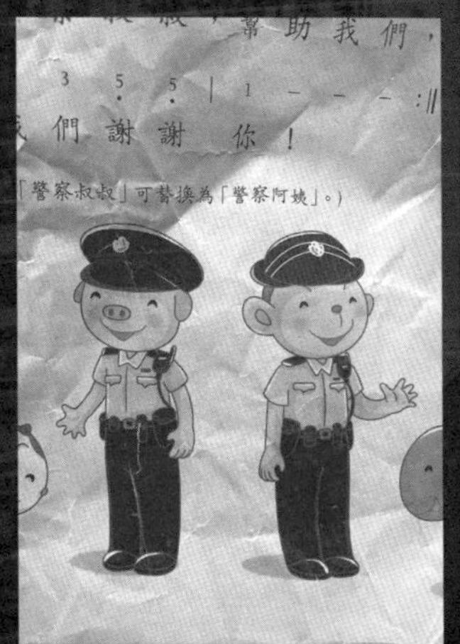
幫助我們，
們謝謝你！
「警察叔叔」可替換為「警察阿姨」。)

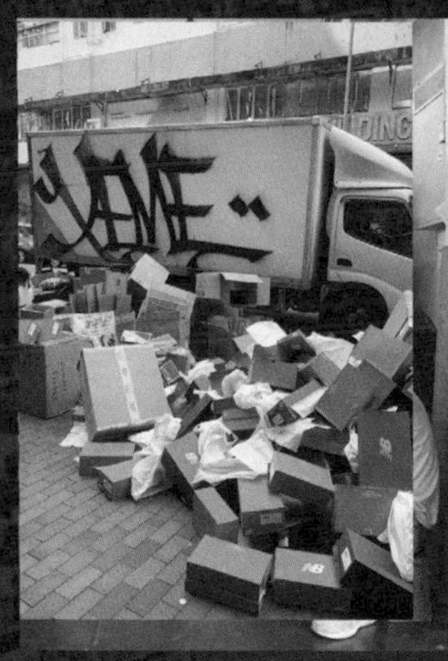
XEME

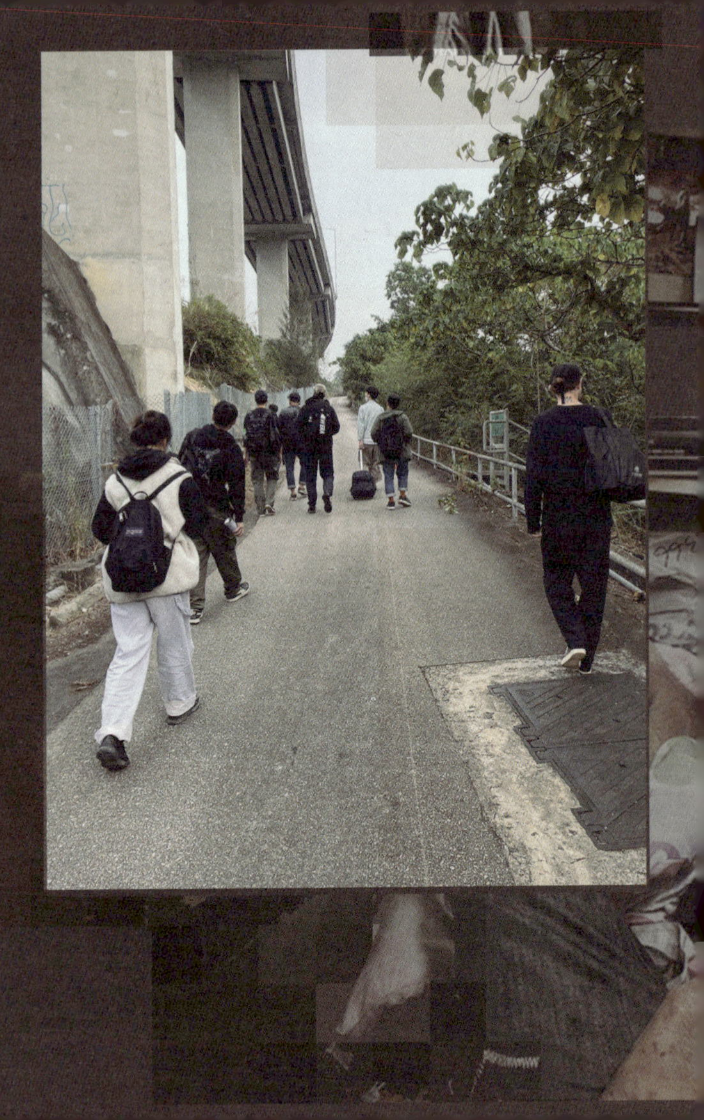

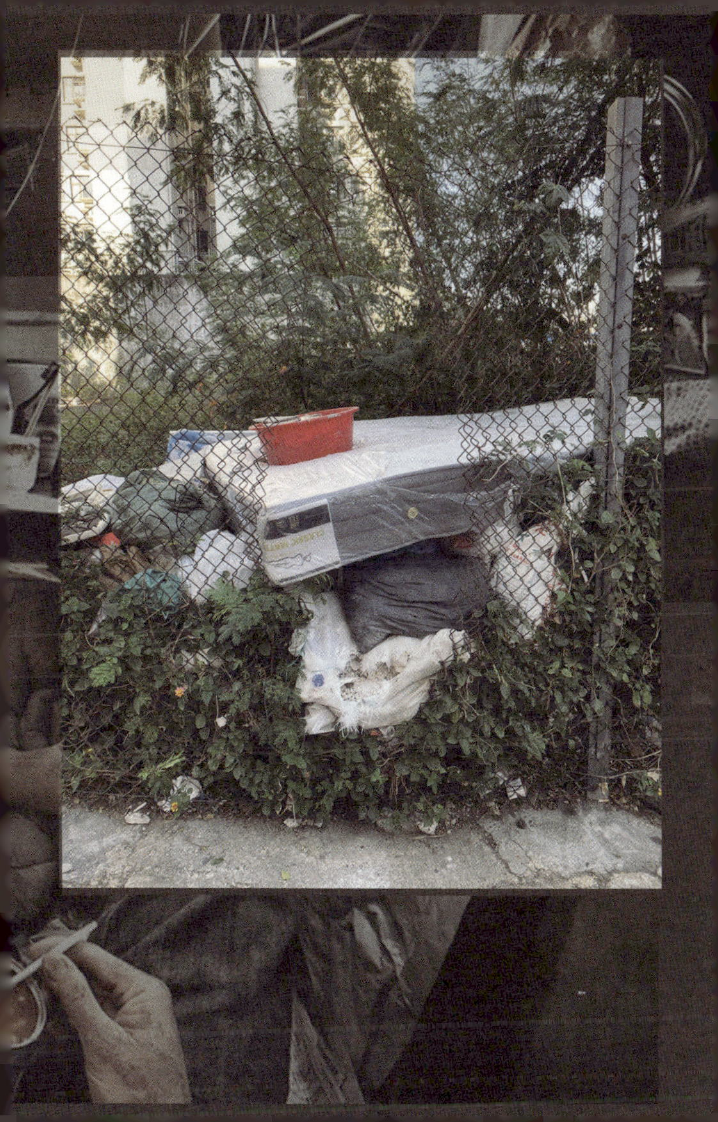

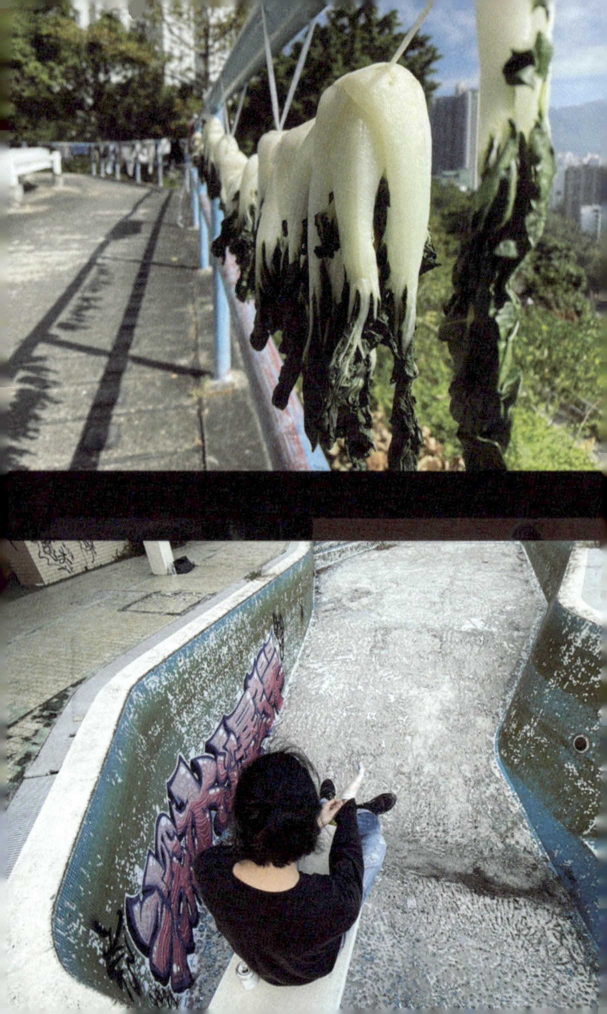

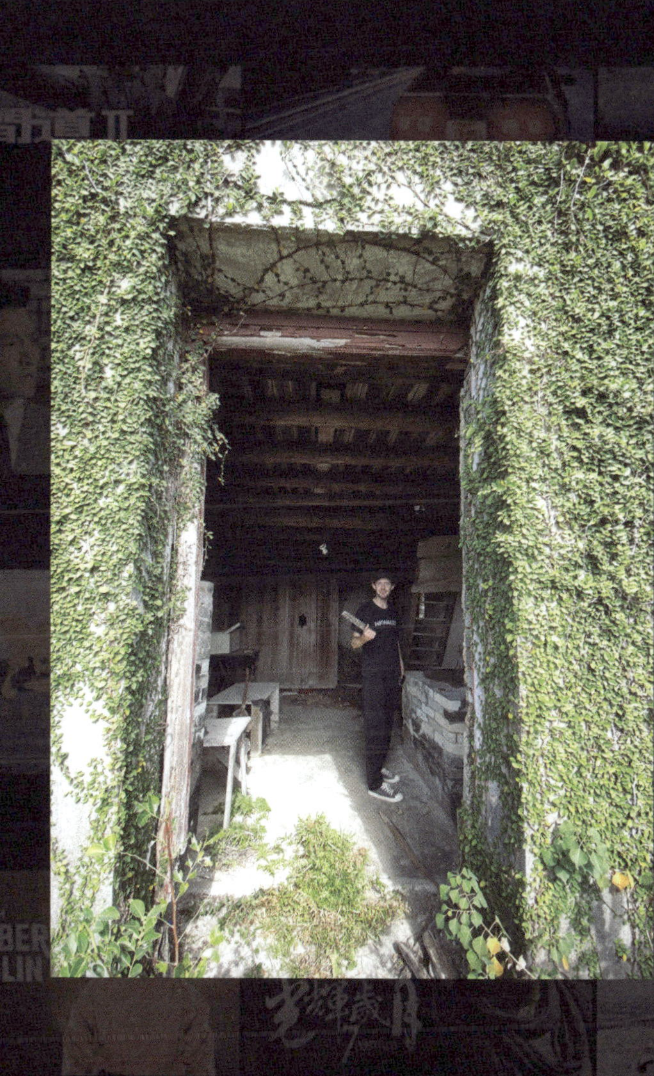

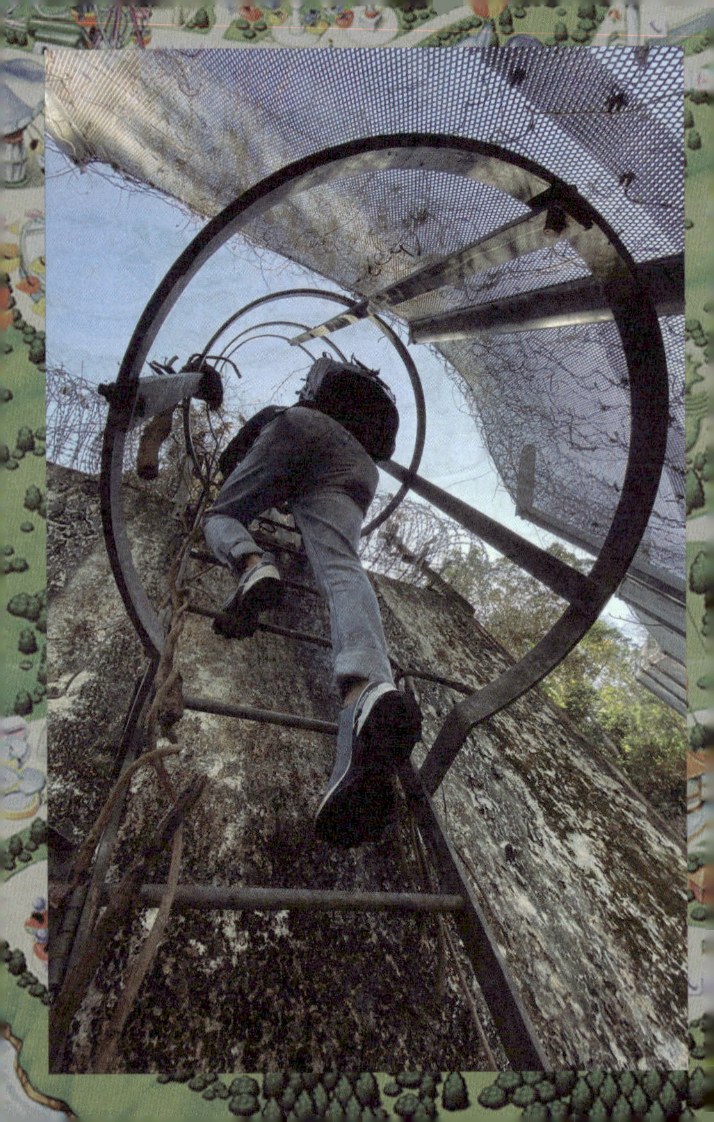

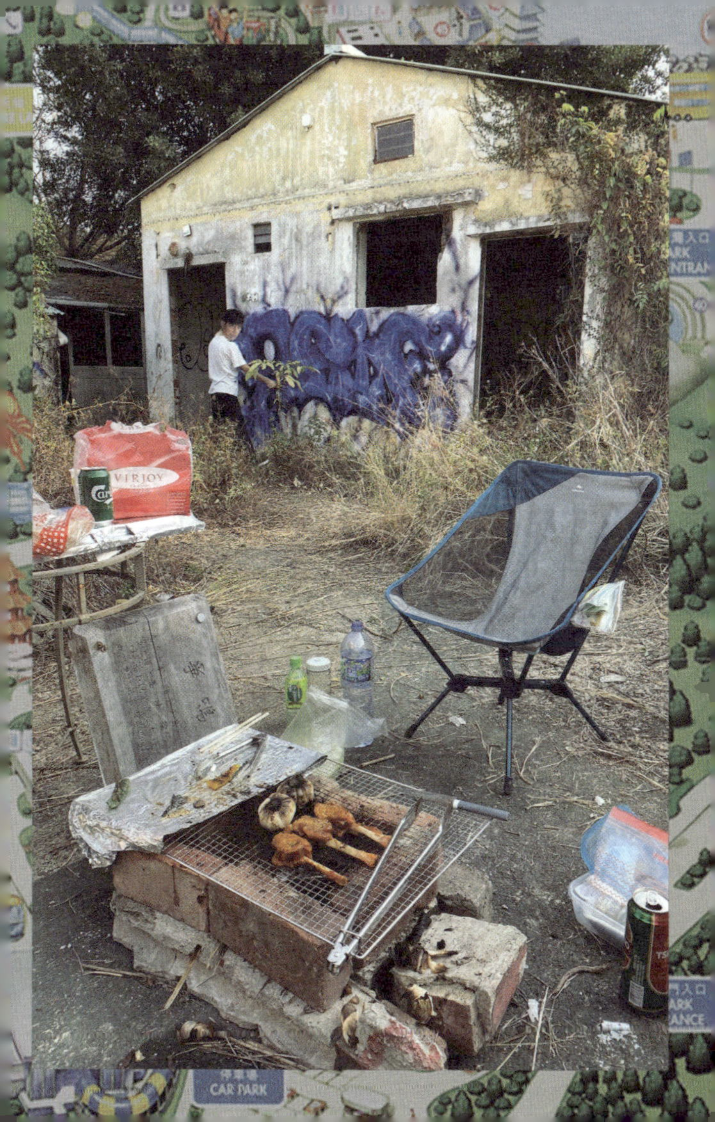
VIRJOY
停車場
CAR PARK

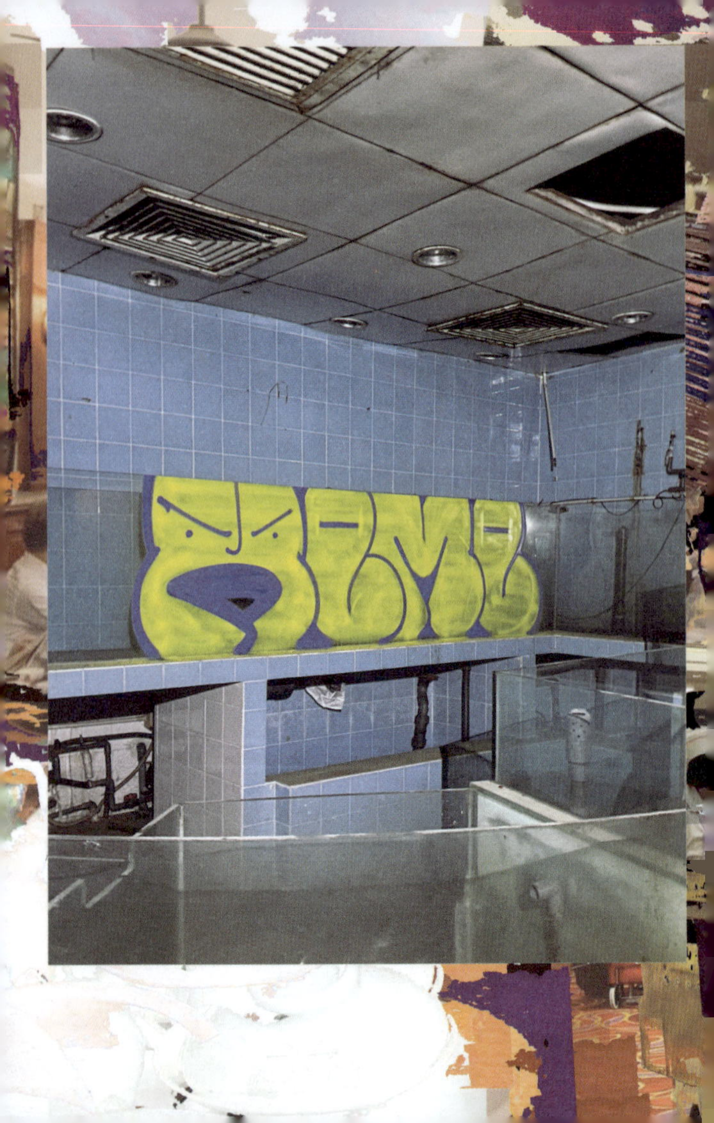

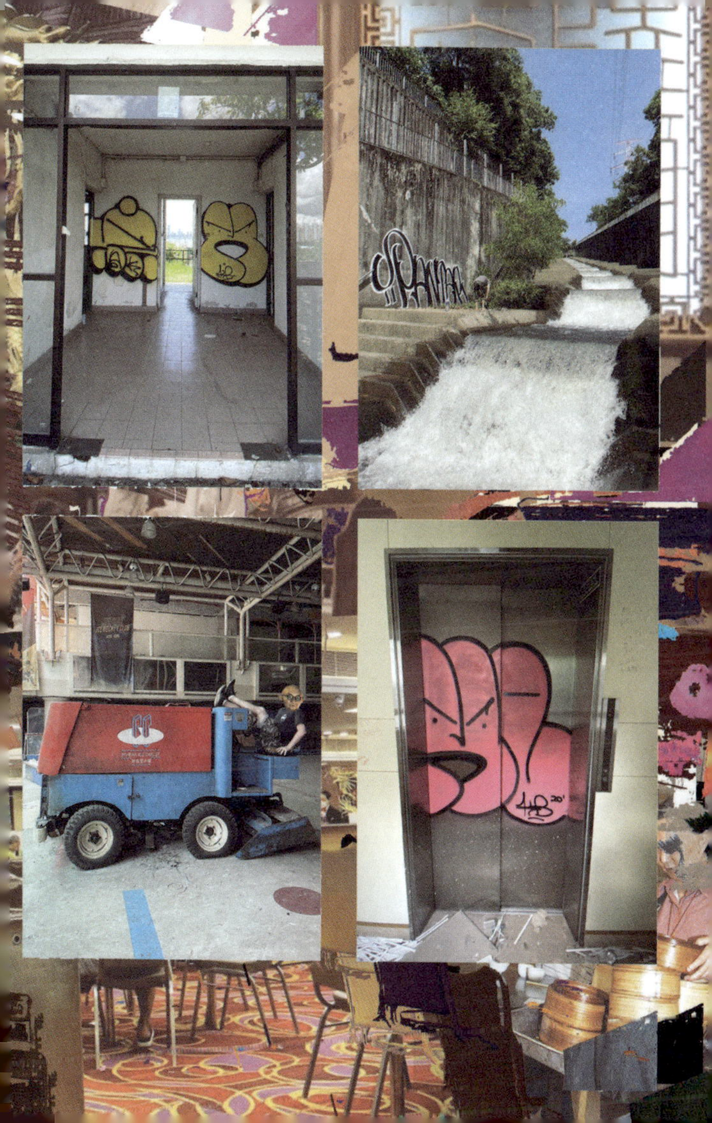

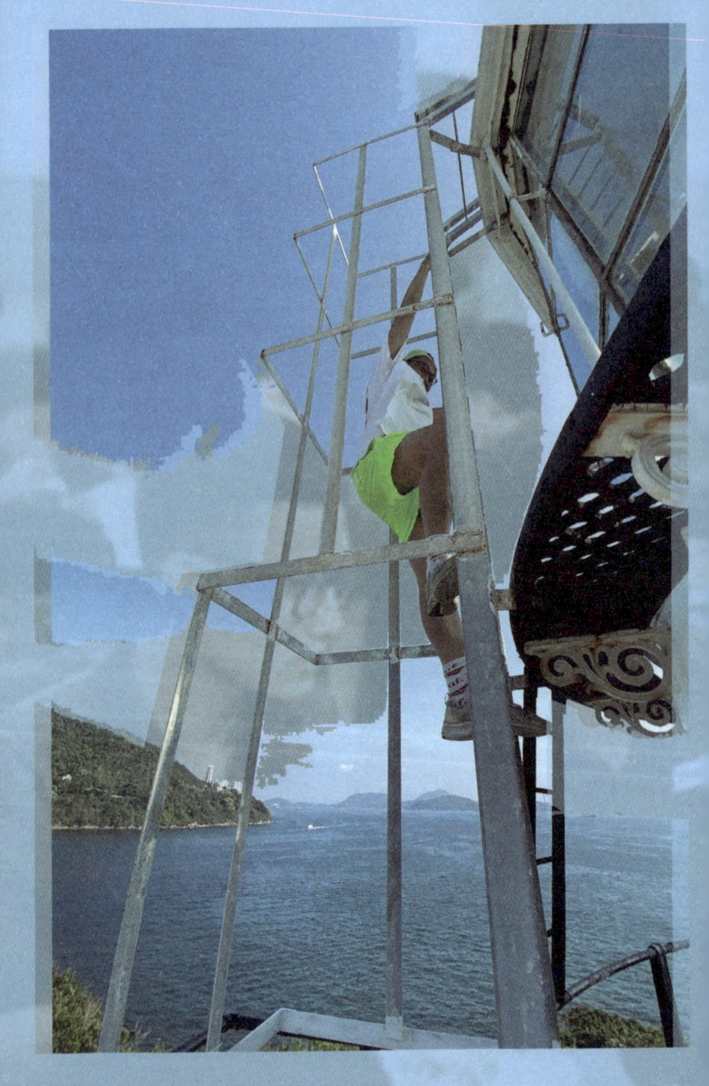

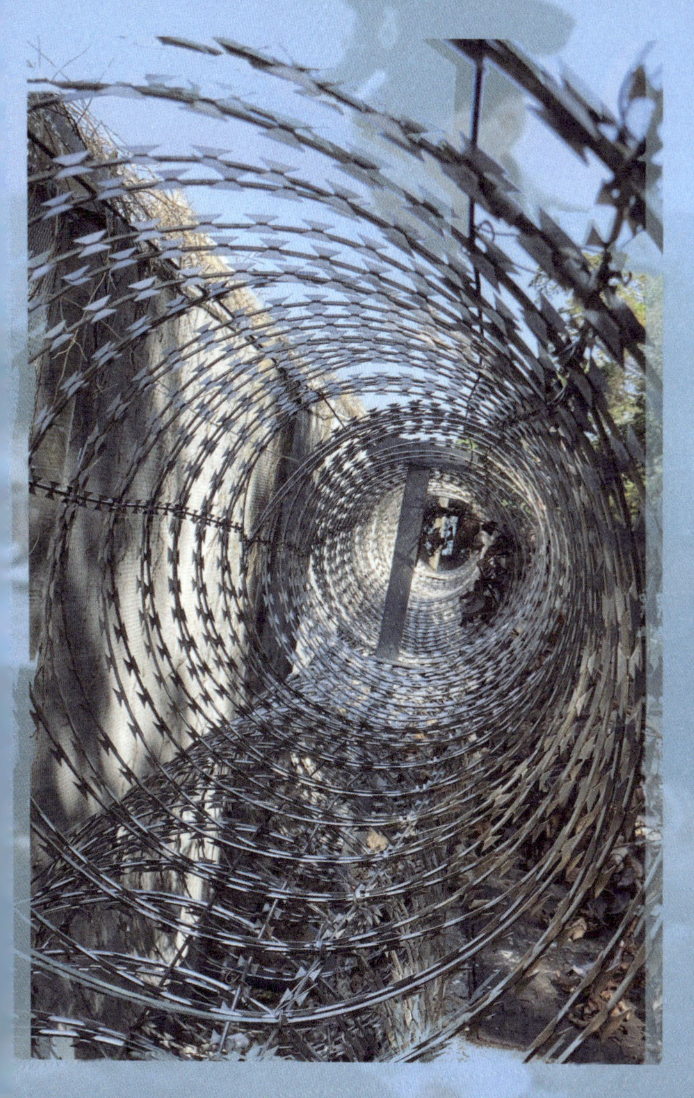

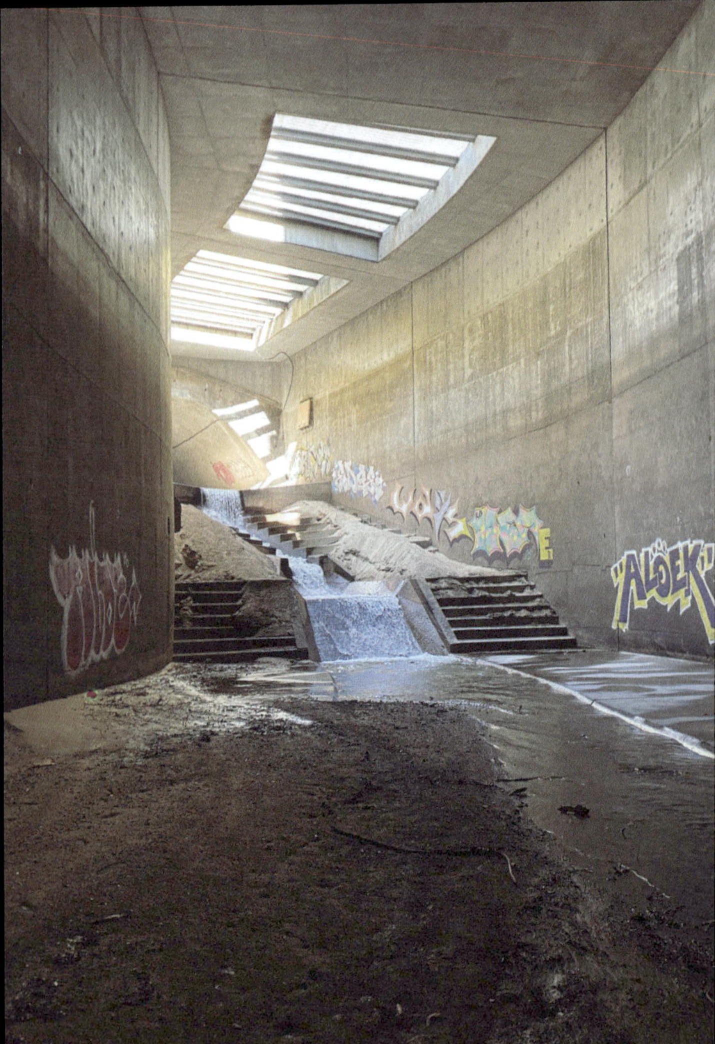
"ALÖEK"

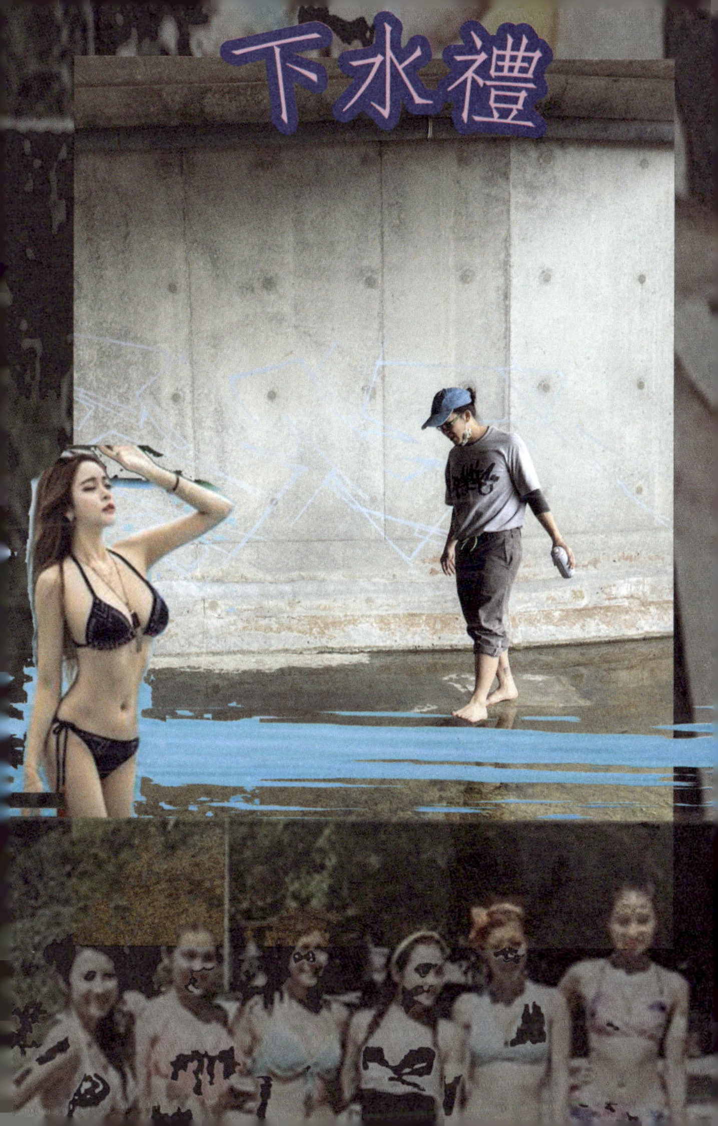
下水禮

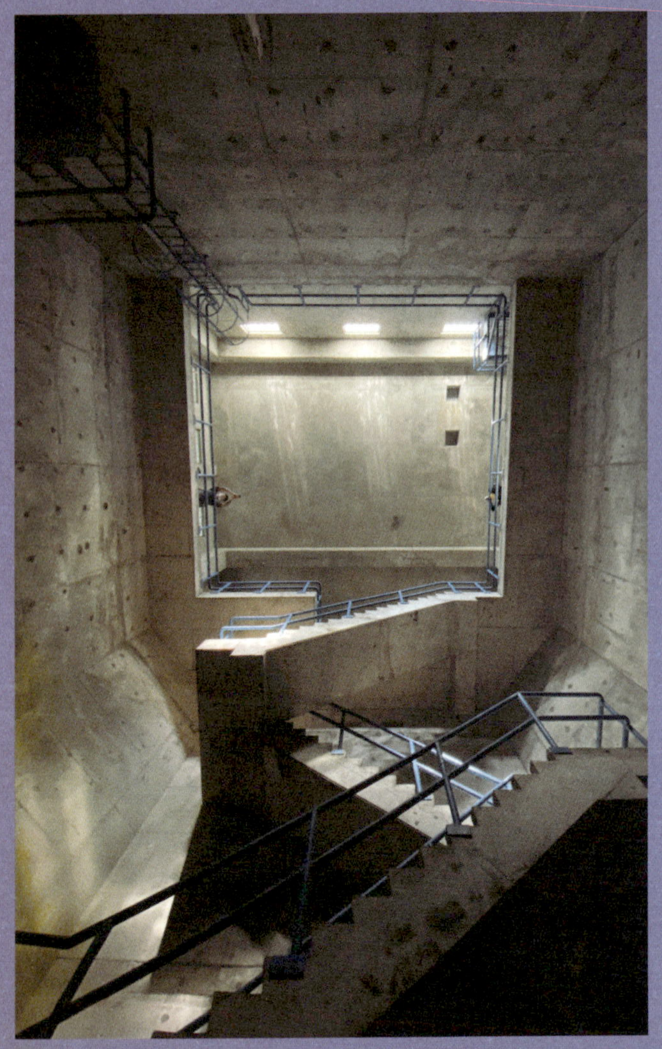

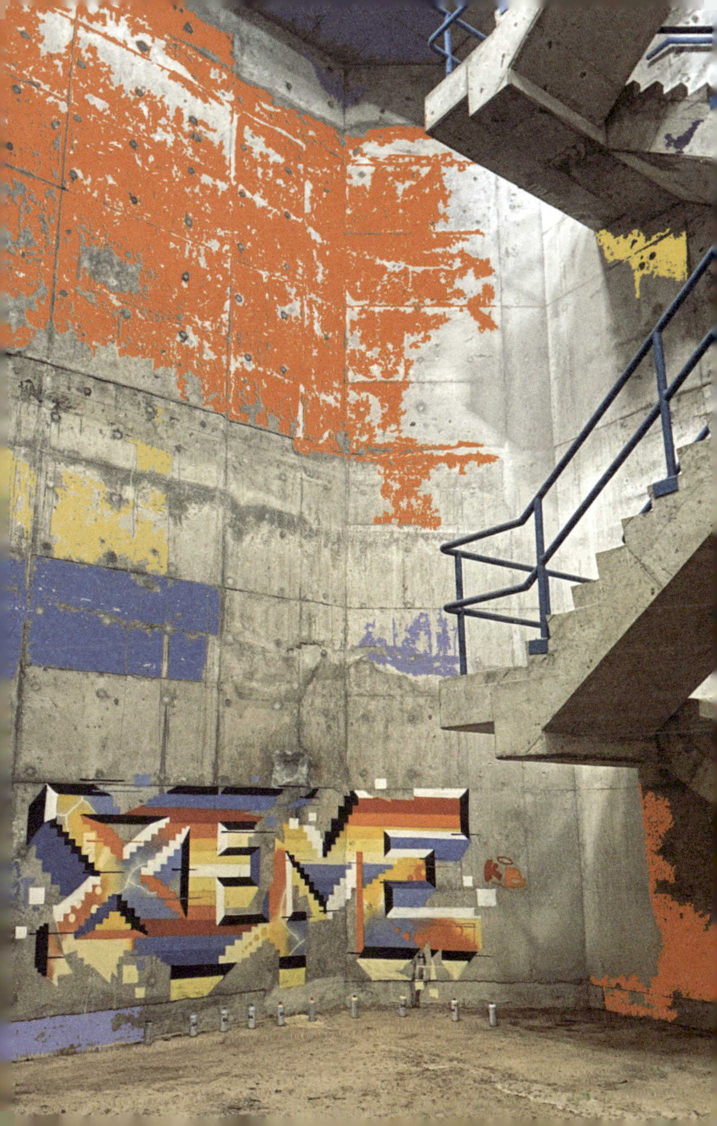

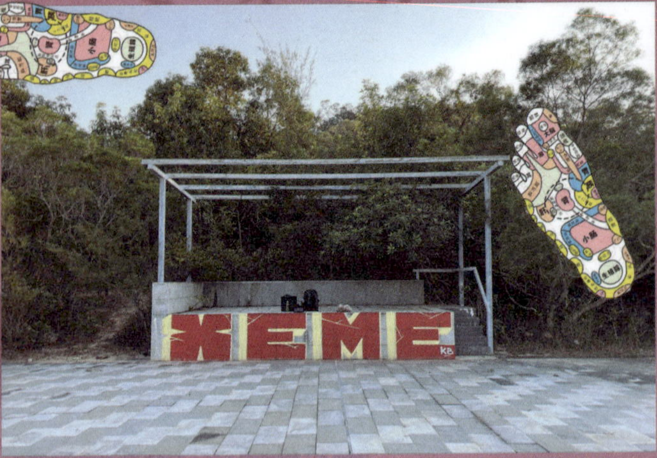

28
38
78
58
80
78
98
58
28
上海式修腳　次
足浴
$13

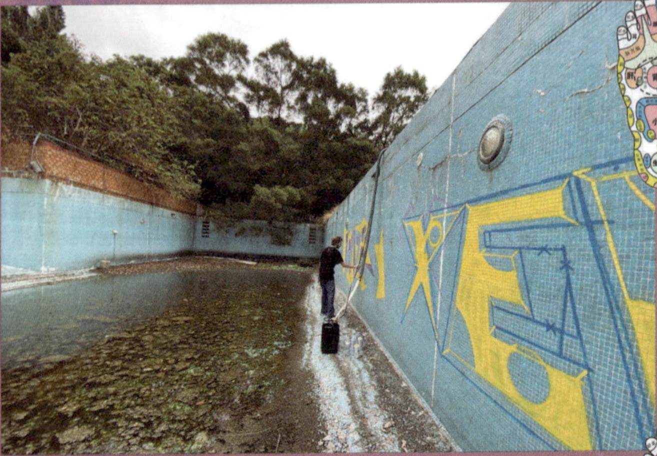

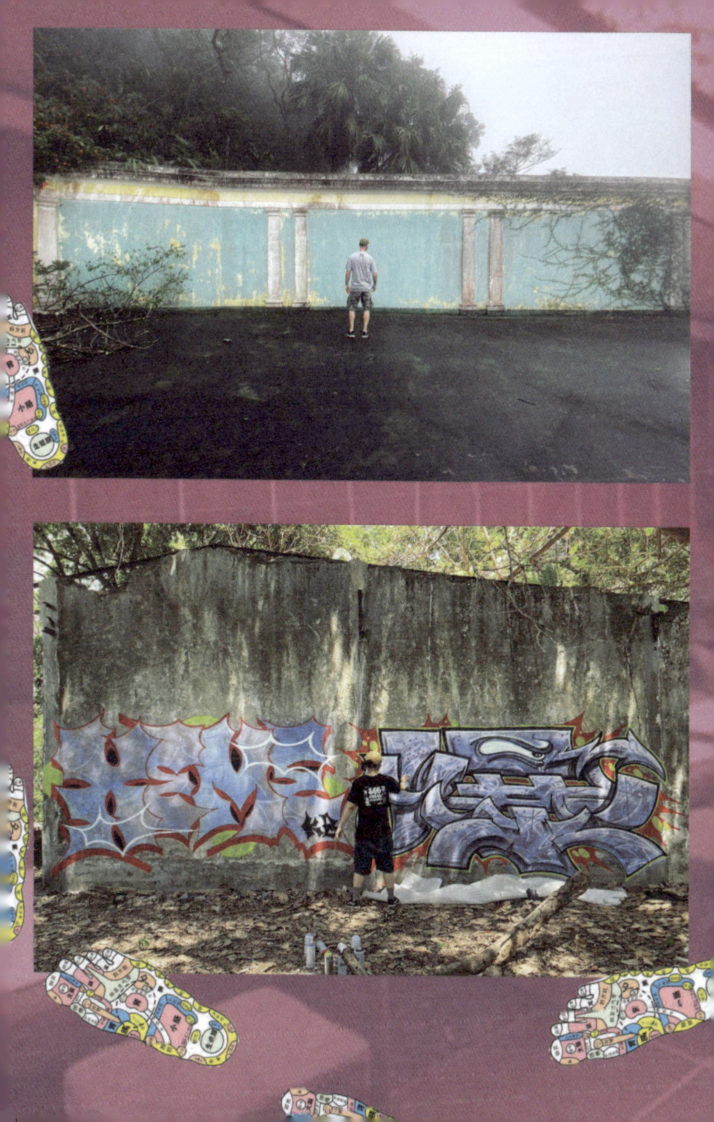

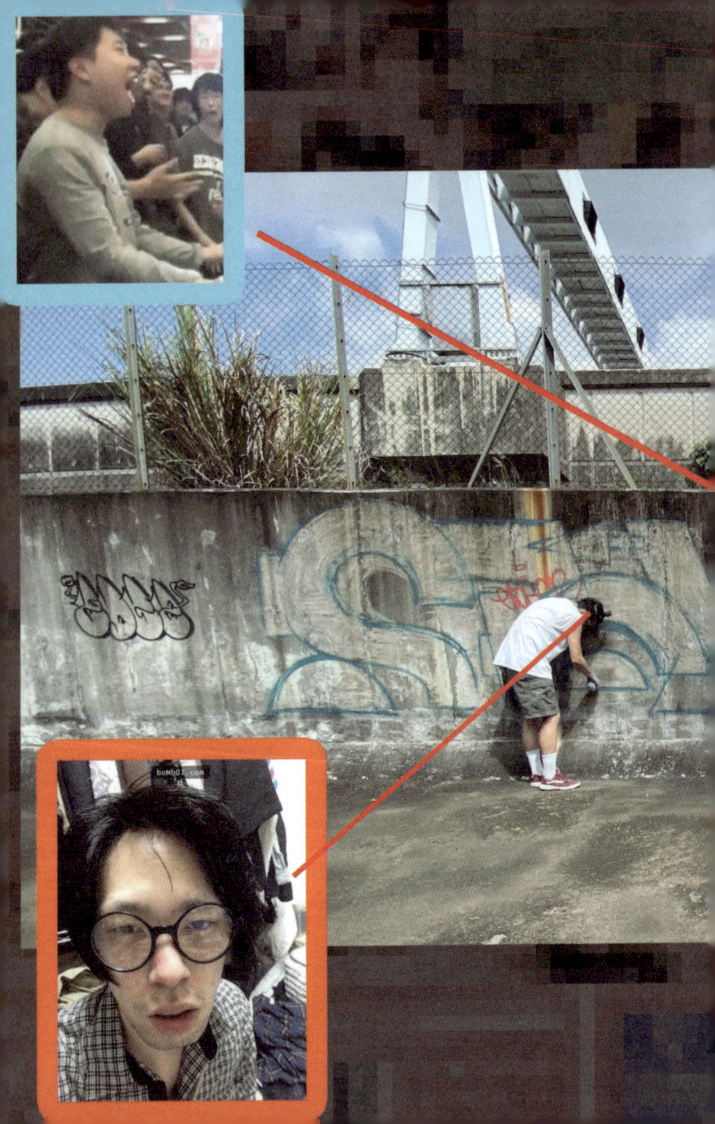

STAY HOME CATS

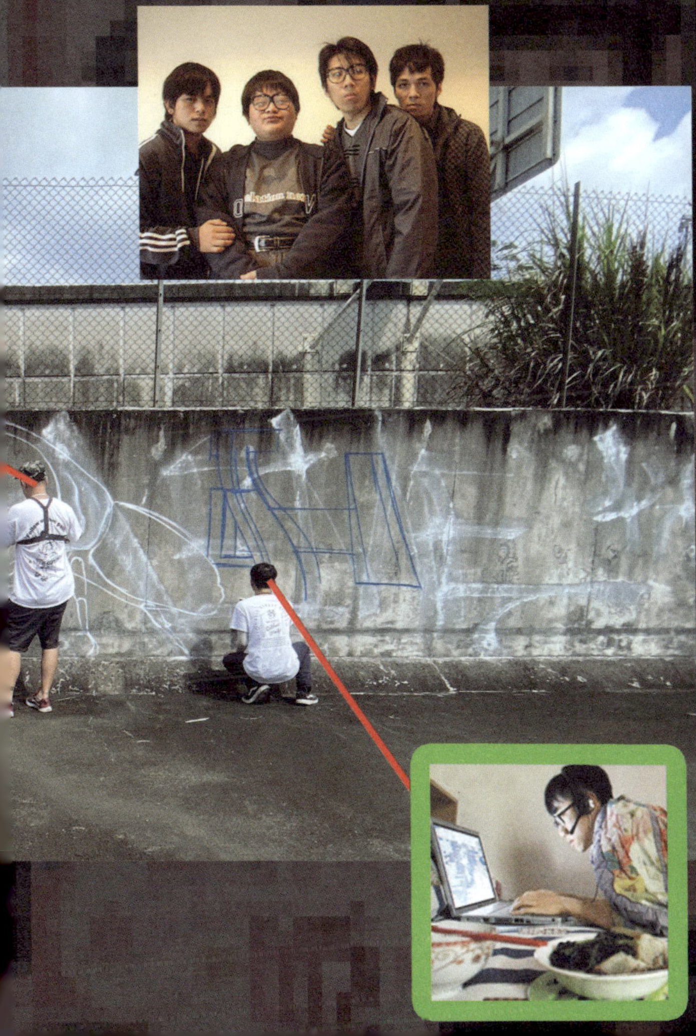

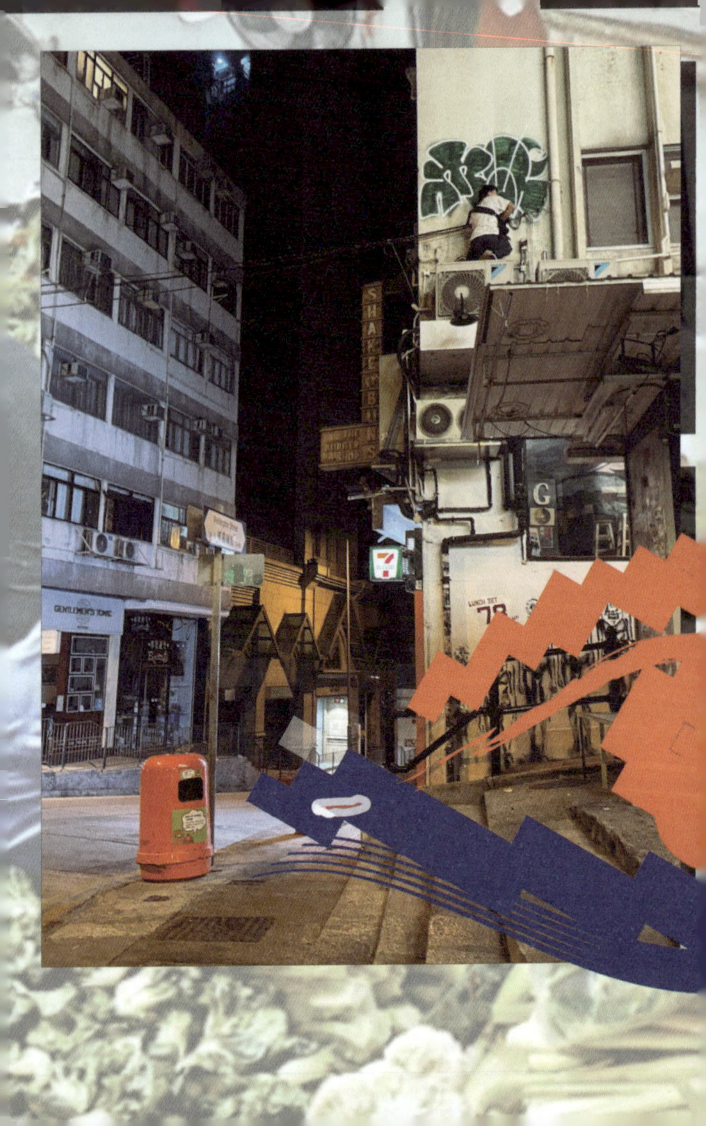
GENTLEMEN'S TONIC
LUNCH SET
78

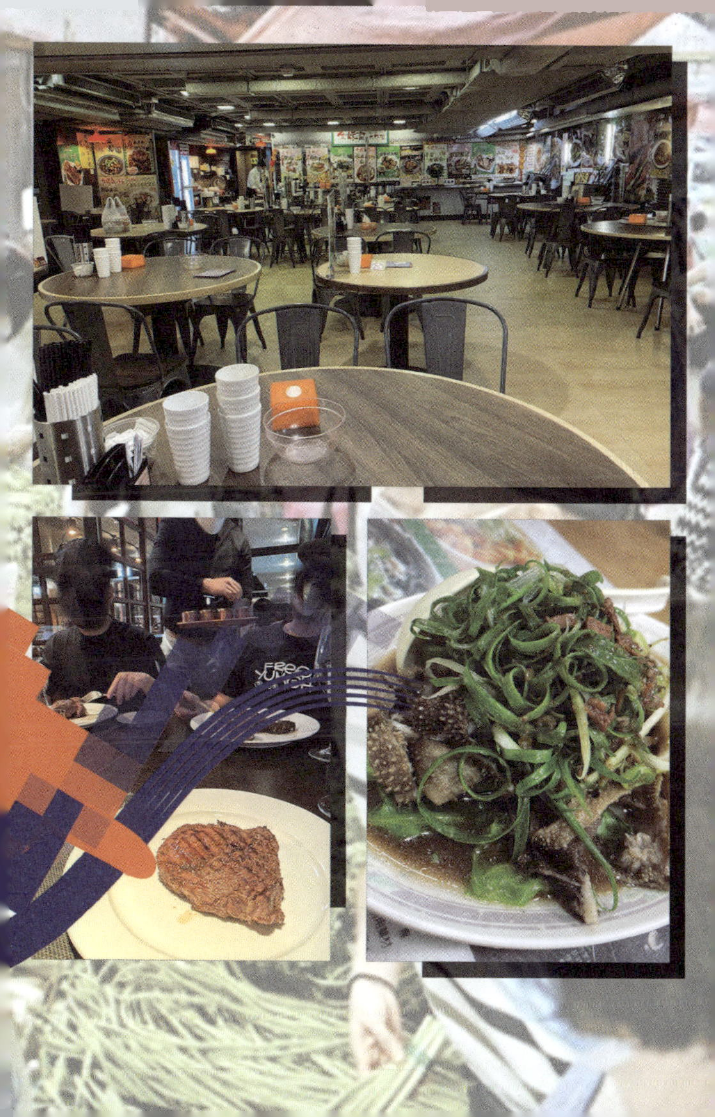

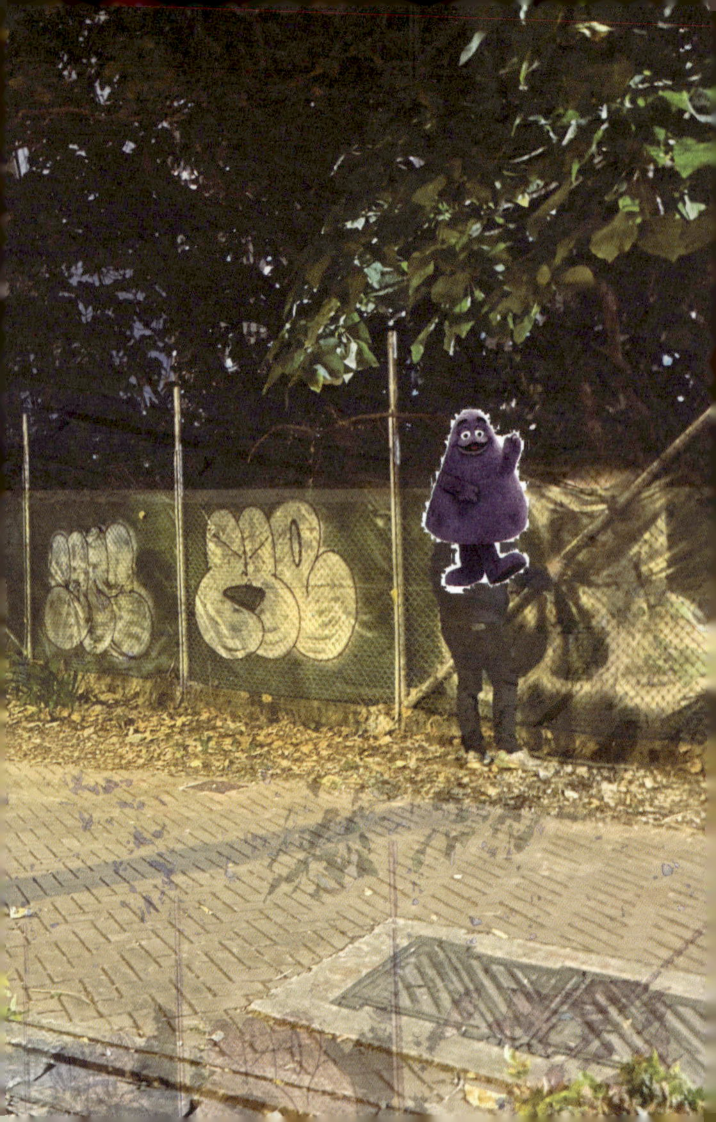

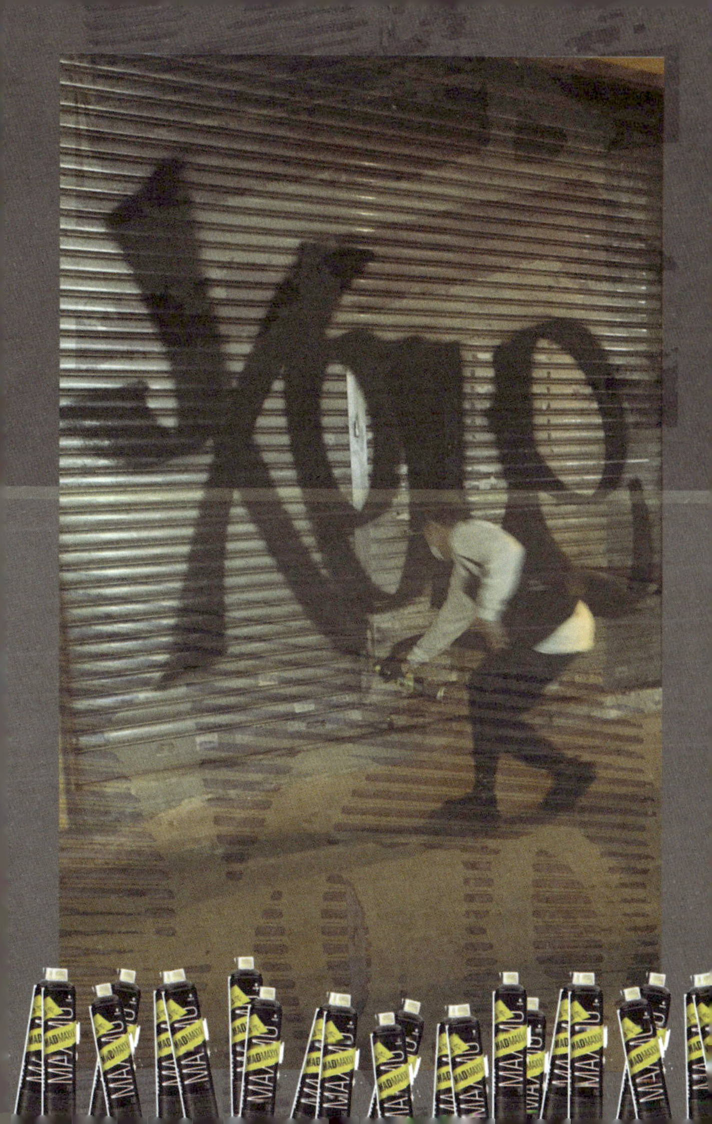

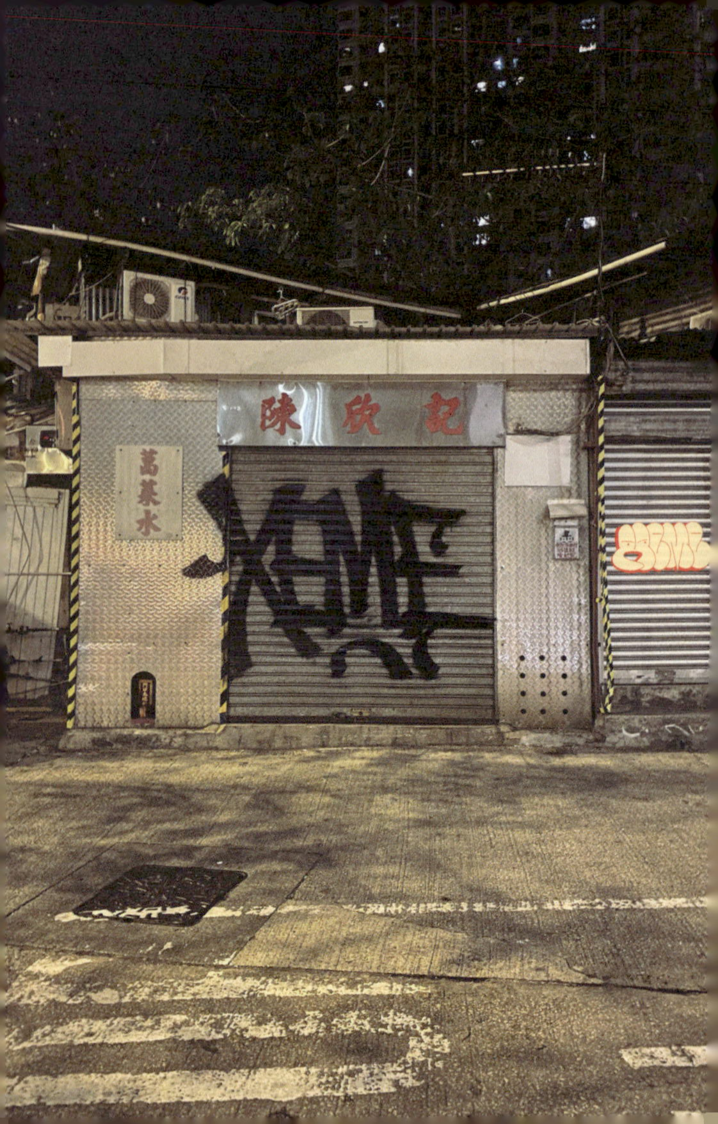
陳欣記

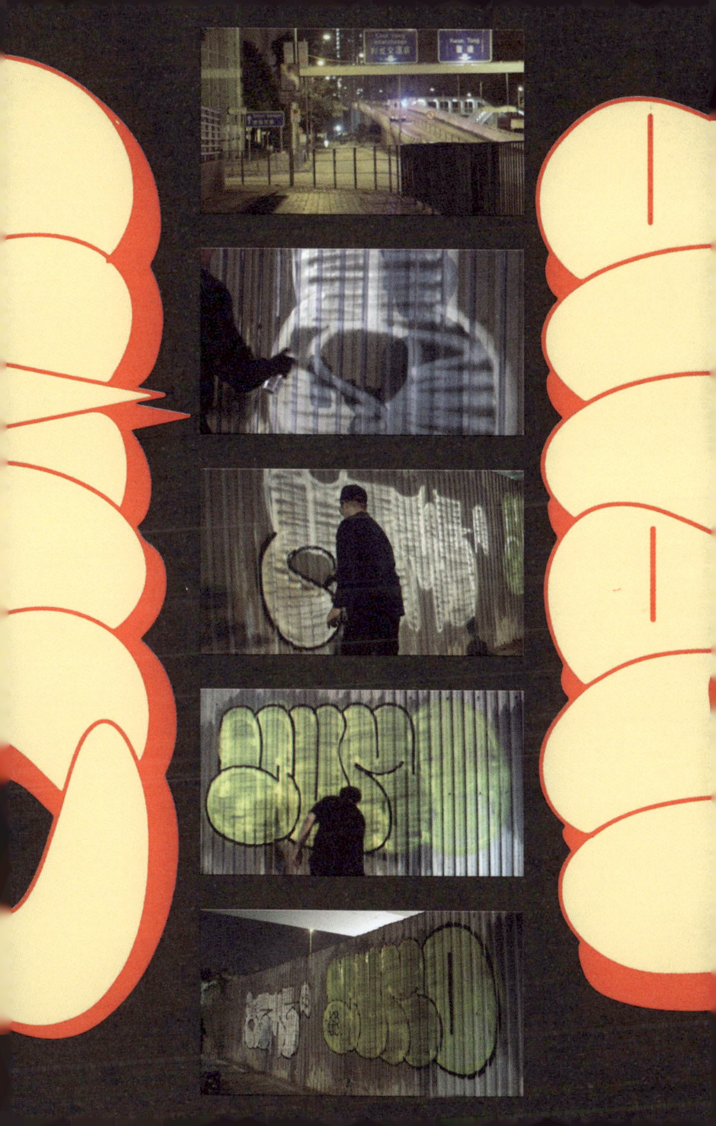

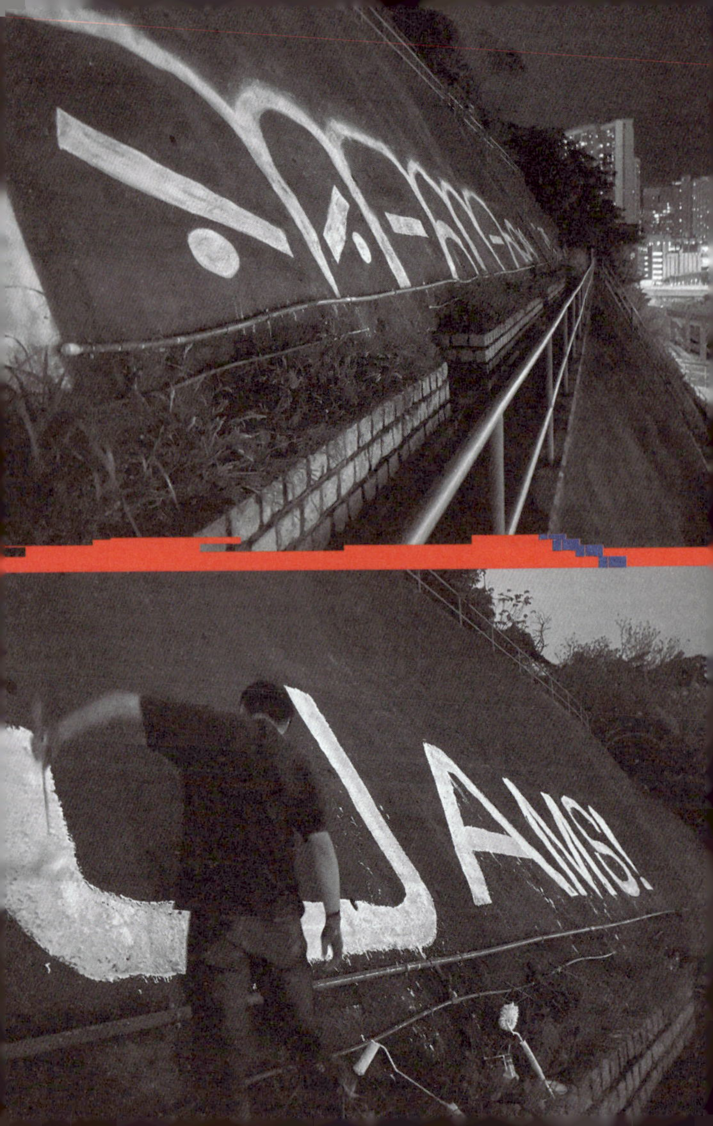

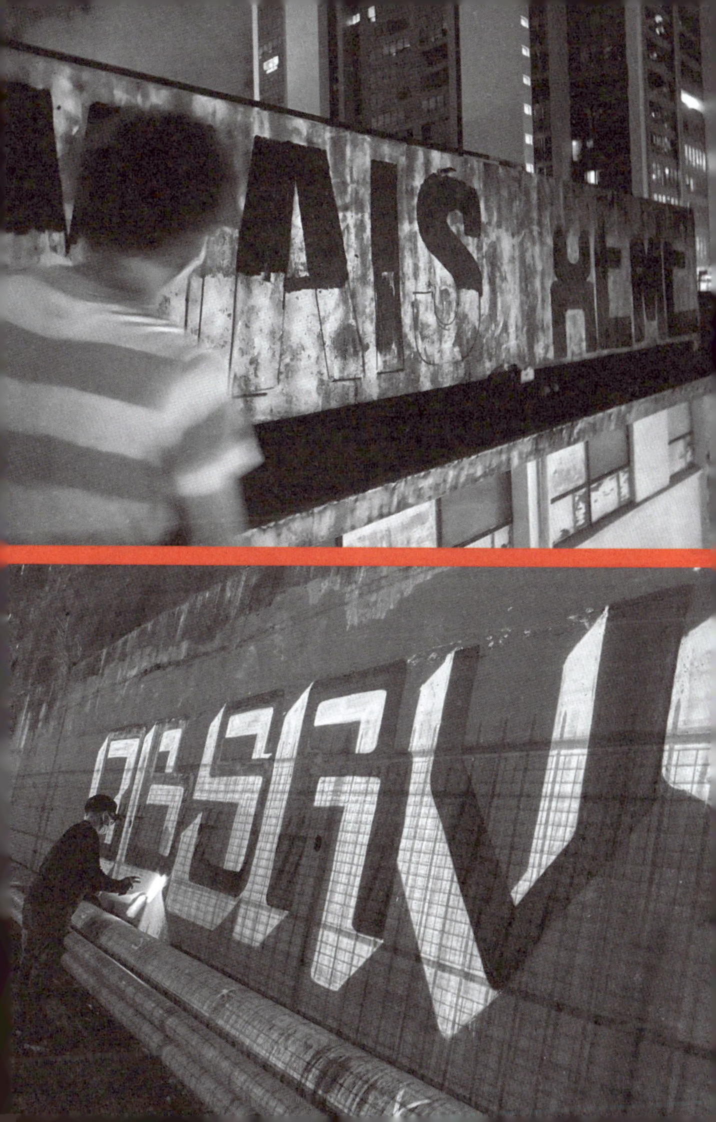

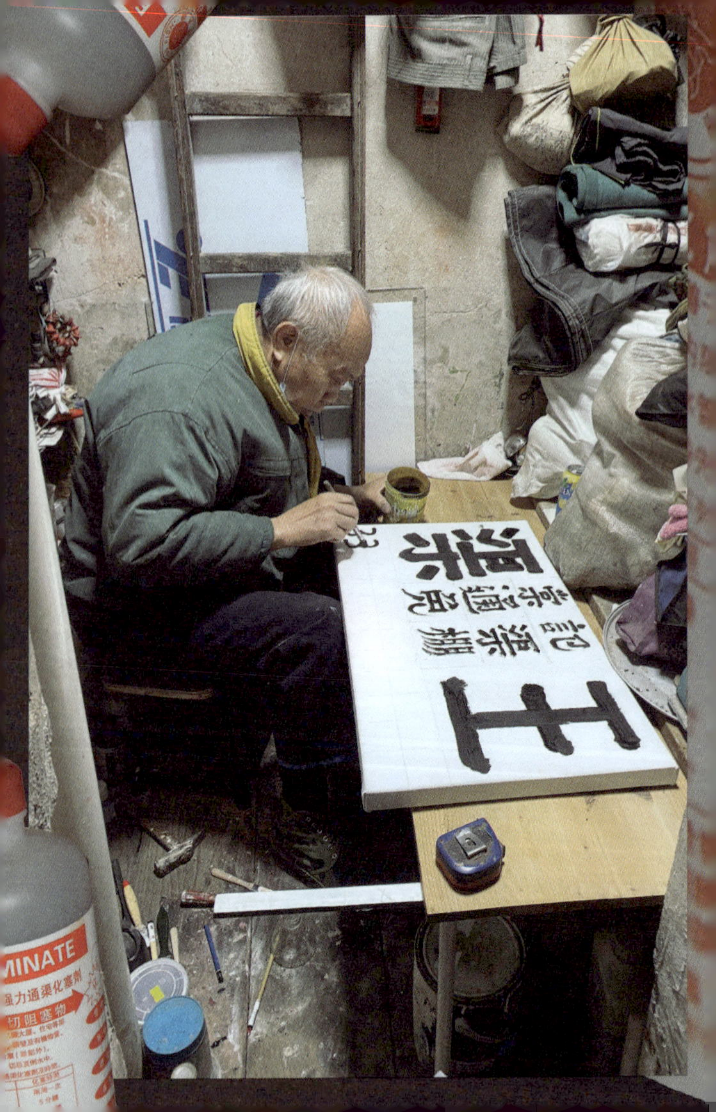
MINATE
强力通渠化塞剂

[10:14 am, 08/12/2021] RYO: So who is that old man in the photo?

[10:18 am, 08/12/2021] XEME: he calls himself "The plumber king". he's actually a really skillful plumber that'll climb out of a 20 floor building and fix your pipes and shit. i started noticing his work (advertisements) since i was a kid. and he'll still ride his scooter around the city and paints his name along with his phone number

[10:18 am, 08/12/2021] XEME: and oh, he's 73 if i'm not wrong

[10:19 am, 08/12/2021] RYO: and he still writes and fixes pipes?

[10:22 am, 08/12/2021] XEME: yeh and he's been putting his name up for decades

[10:30 am, 08/12/2021] XEME: i'd go see him from time to time just to chit chat and say hi

[10:30 am, 08/12/2021] XEME: he'd called me up sometimes saying he painted a dope spot. so he's kinda like a graff person

[10:30 am, 08/12/2021] RYO: What!! haha

[10:31 am, 08/12/2021] RYO: So his mentality is actually 'graff'. So he gets what the younger graffiti writers are doing then

[10:33 am, 08/12/2021] XEME: a little but not a lot. he can't really read our tags or throws but he'll remember the shape of it, the little doodads

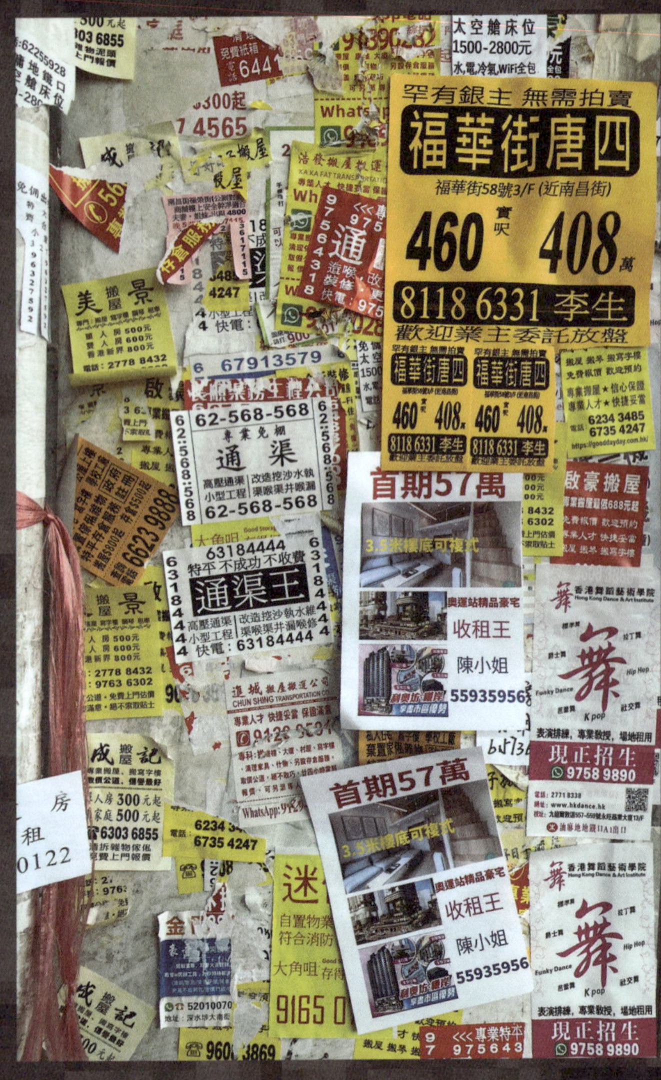

太空艙床位
1500-2800元
水電冷氣WiFi全包
罕有銀主 無需拍賣
福華街唐四
福華街58號3/F (近南昌街)
460 實呎 408萬
8118 6331 李生
歡迎業主委託放盤
美景搬屋
單人房 500元
雙人房 600元
香港新界 800元
電話：2778 8432
67913579
62-568-568
專業免棚
通渠
高壓通渠 改造挖沙水執
小型工程 渠喉渠井喉漏
62-568-568
63184444
特平不成功不收費
通渠王
高壓通渠 改造挖沙執水維
小型工程 渠喉渠井漏喉修
快電：63184444
首期57萬
3.5米樓底可複式
奧運站精品豪宅
收租王
陳小姐
55935956
啟豪搬屋
香港舞蹈藝術學院
Hong Kong Dance & Art Institute
舞
Hip Hop
Funky Dance
K pop
表演排練，專業教授，場地租用
現正招生
9758 9890
6234 3485
6735 4247
成記搬屋
6303 6855
9165
<<< 專業特平
975643

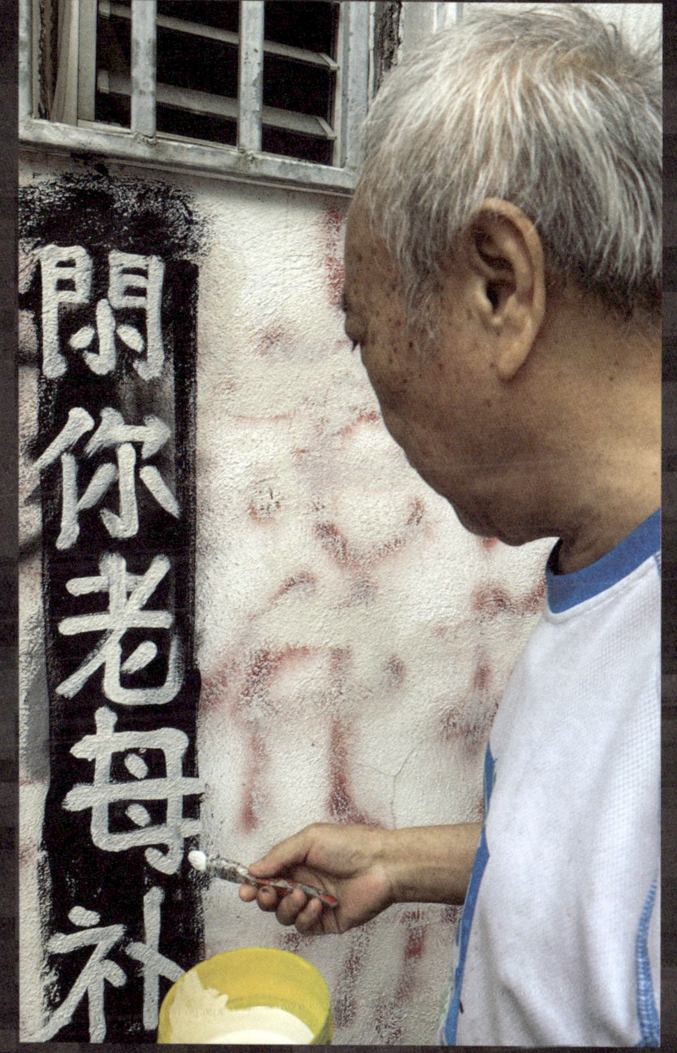

閄你老母补

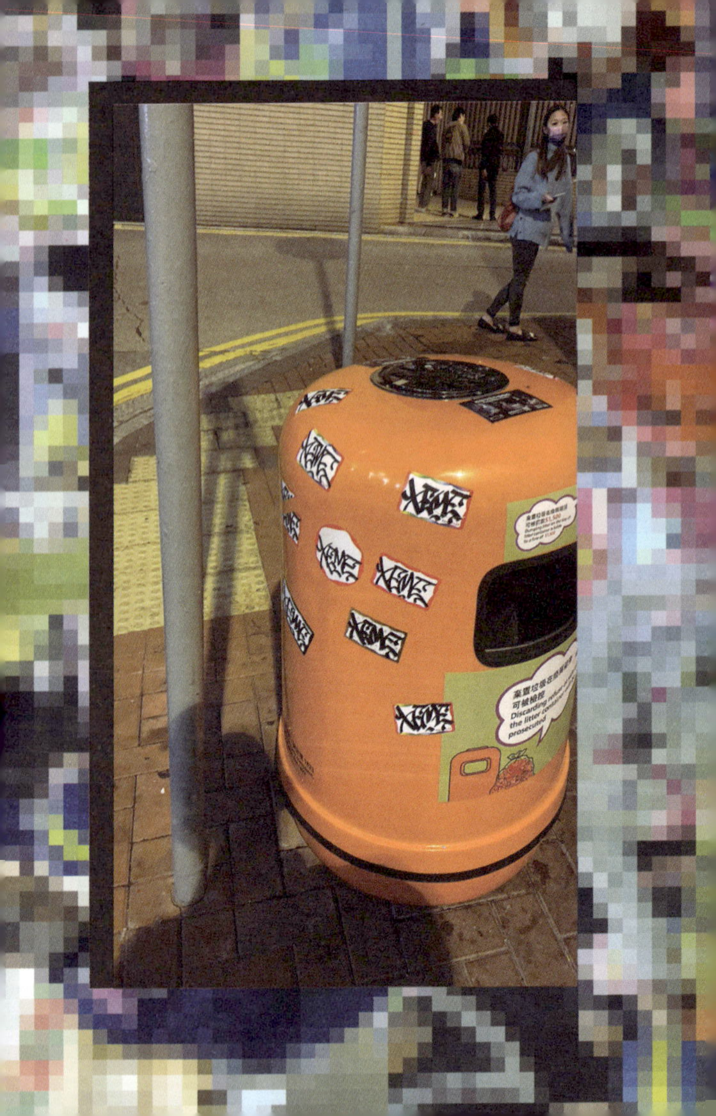
棄置垃圾在
可被檢控
Discarding
the litter
prosecuted

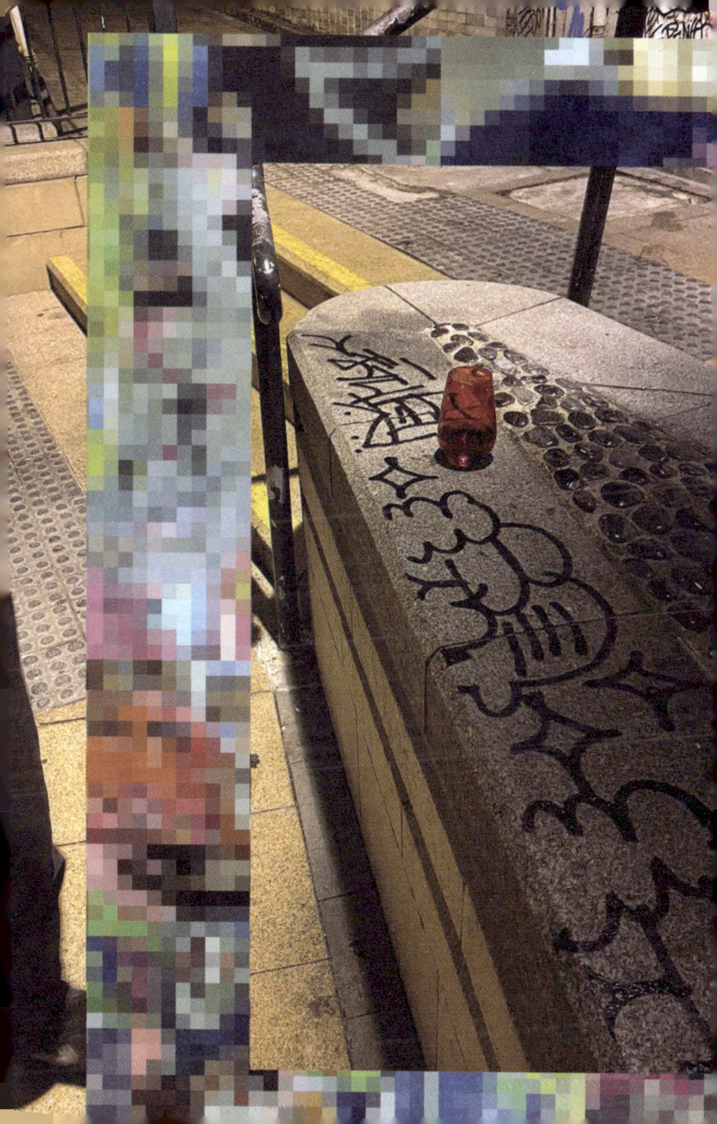

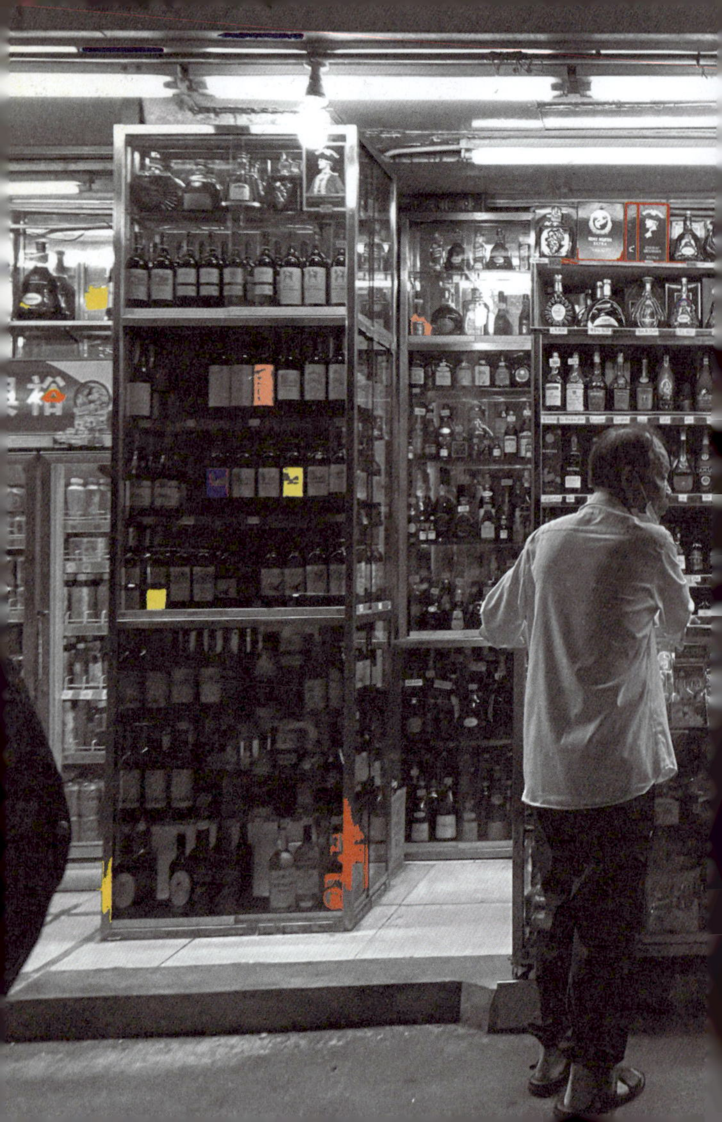
裕

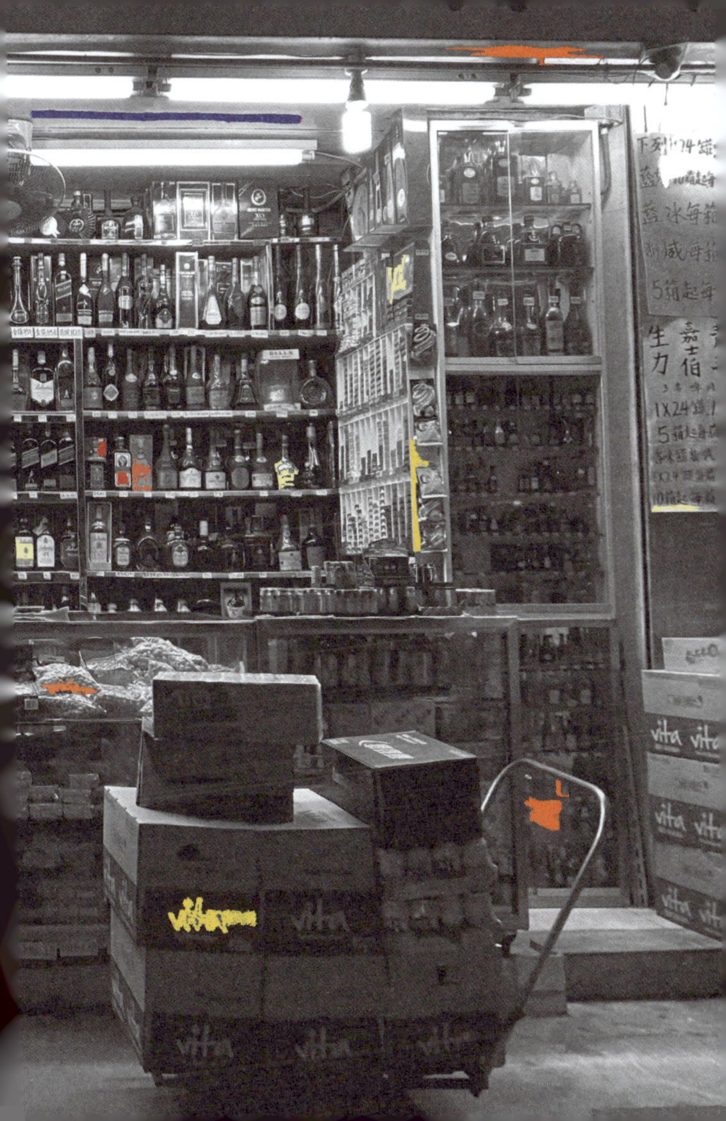
vita

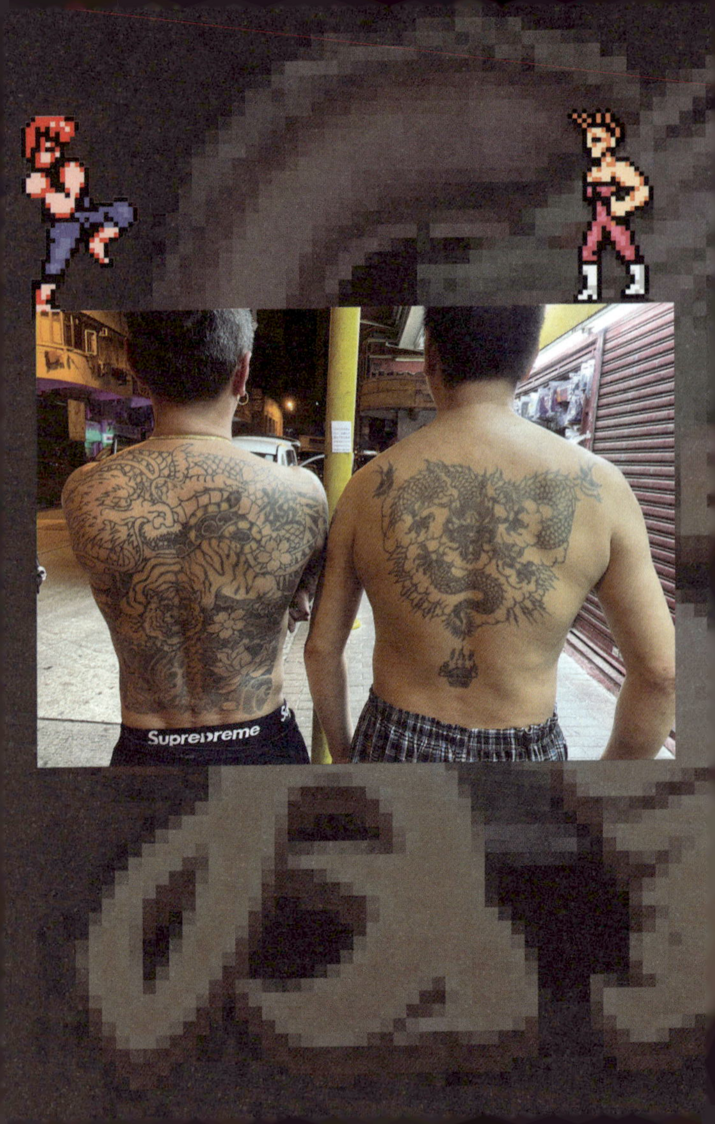

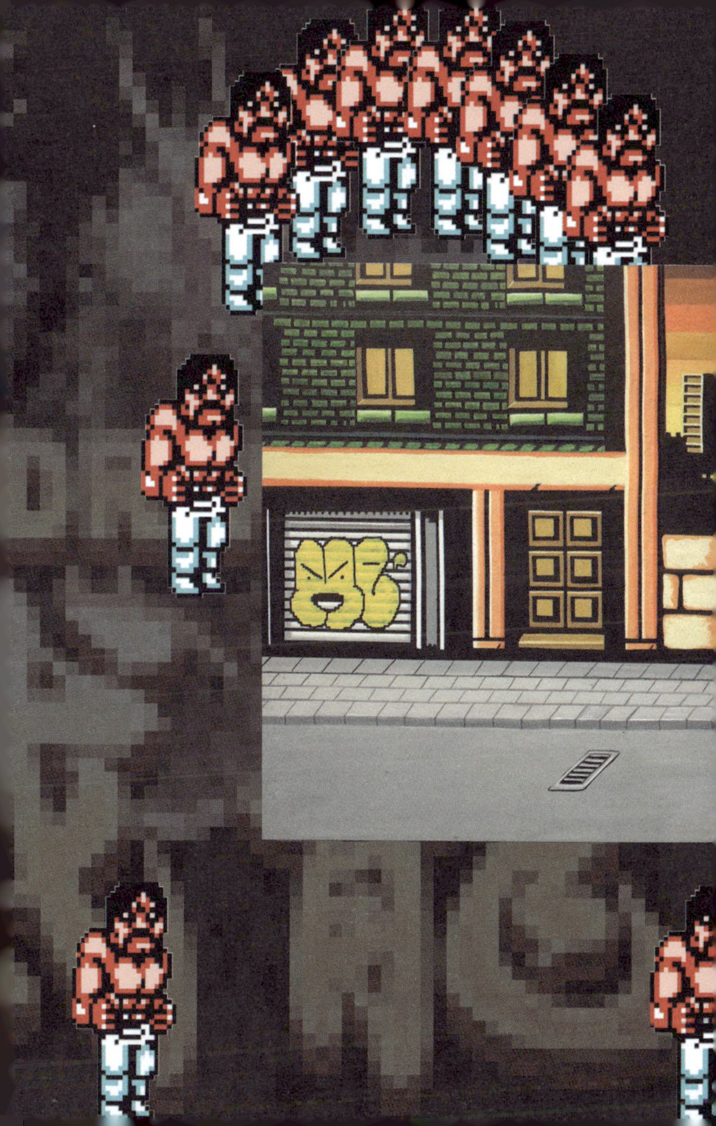

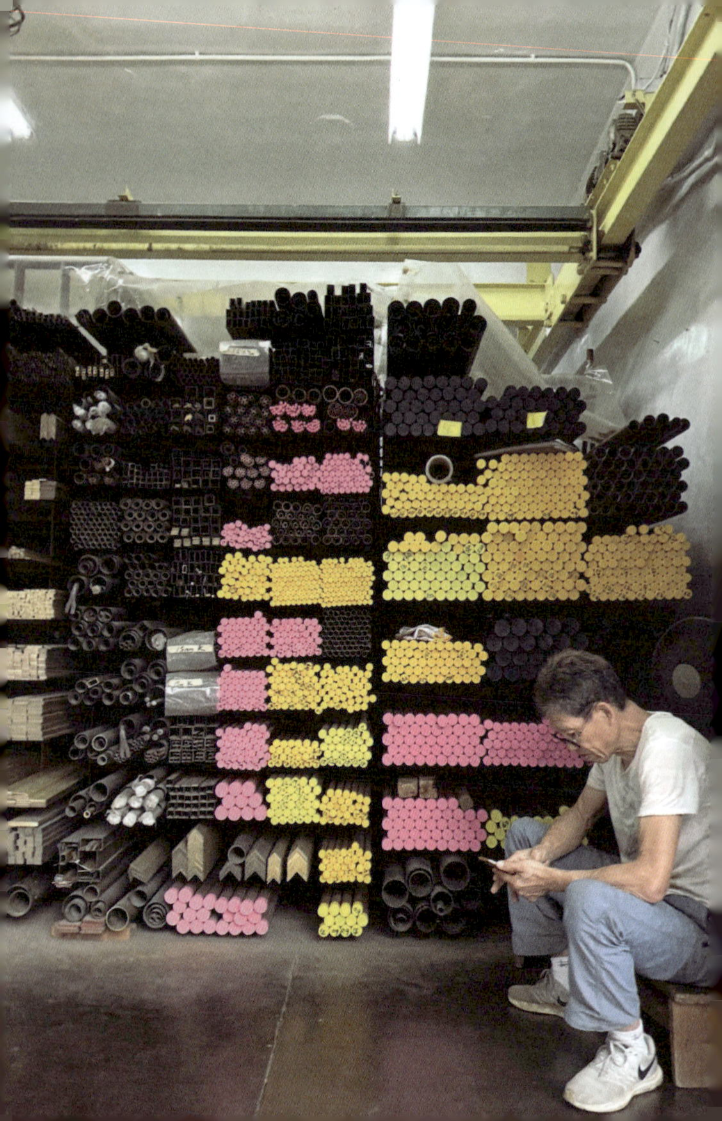

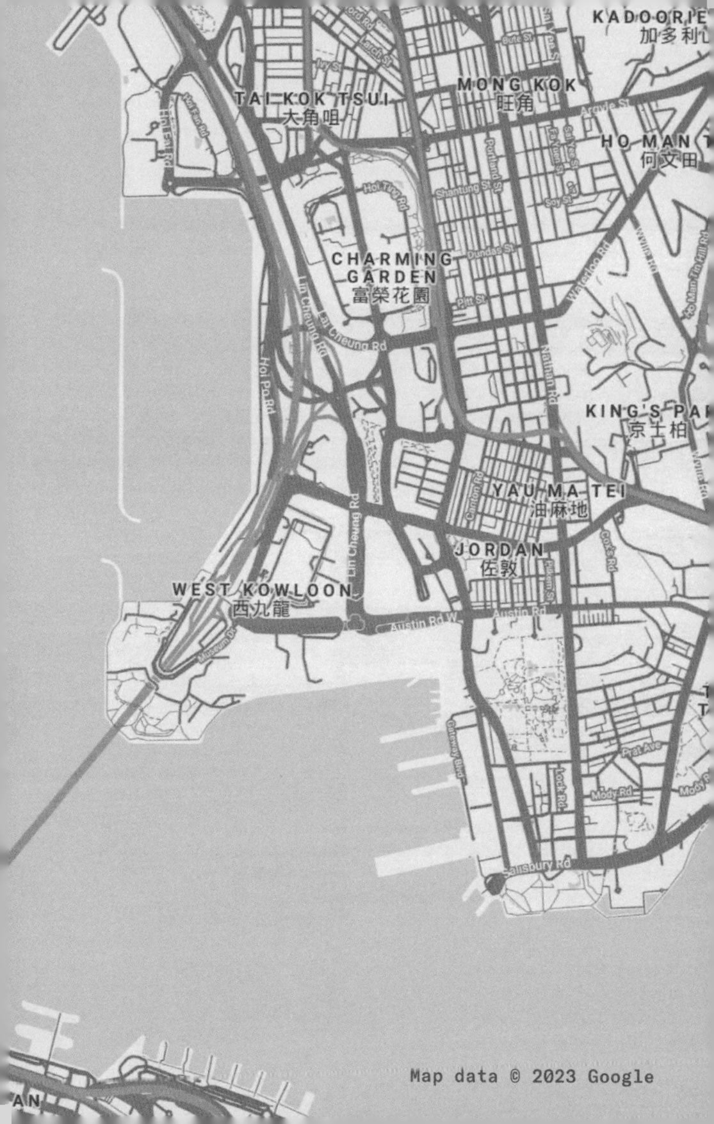
KADOORIE
MONG KOK
旺角
TAI KOK TSUI
大角咀
Argyle St
何文田
Portland St
Shantung St
Hoi Ting Rd
CHARMING
GARDEN
富榮花園
Dundas St
Pitt St
Waterloo Rd
Lin Cheung Rd
Lai Cheung Rd
Hoi Po Rd
Nathan Rd
京士柏
YAU MA TEI
油麻地
Canton Rd
Lin Cheung Rd
JORDAN
佐敦
Cox's Rd
WEST KOWLOON
西九龍
Austin Rd W
Austin Rd
Prat Ave
Mody Rd
Lock Rd
Salisbury Rd
Map data © 2023 Google